Dearest ~~~~~
Choice No: 1
wedding ~~~~
It doesn't s~~~~ ~~~~
Lots of love ~~~~ ~~~~~

Truth *or* Dare

A BOOK OF SECRETS SHARED

Truth *or* Dare

A BOOK OF SECRETS SHARED

Commissioned and edited by Justine Picardie

PICADOR

First published 2004 by Picador
an imprint of Pan Macmillan Ltd
Pan Macmillan, 20 New Wharf Road, London N1 9RR
Basingstoke and Oxford
Associated companies throughout the world
www.panmacmillan.com

ISBN 0 330 43479 9 (hardback)

1 3 5 7 9 8 6 4 2

A CIP catalogue record for this book is available
from the British Library.

Typeset by SetSystems Ltd, Saffron Walden, Essex
Printed and bound in Great Britain by
Mackays of Chatham plc, Chatham, Kent

Contents

Introduction Justine Picardie

I am sitting on a top bunk with my younger sister and our best friend, Simon; sometimes we're in the bedroom that Ruth and I share, sometimes we're at Simon's house, while our mothers talk to each other downstairs, low murmurs that do not reach us here. Or if we're not in the bedroom, we're on a garden wall or a climbing frame outside – always the highest place we can find, because we're playing truth or dare, a game that involves a leap into danger; and yet it's liberating, too, a bid for freedom, which is why we return to it over and over again.

You must know the rules of the game – we all do – whereby the telling of a truth (a secret by any other name) may be more dangerous than the alternative act of daring. In fact, the revelation of truth is in itself a kind of dare – turning yourself inside out, letting the world hear the beating of your heart. What is more frightening: to kiss Simon, or jump off the top bunk, or to admit to loving him?

As children, we abided by the rules: the truth was always told (if truth was the choice we had made that day); a lie was never substituted; a secret was only a secret, because it contained within it the potential to be shared. That's how it seemed to me, anyway, as if there might be some awful retribution if we sacrificed truthfulness for an easy life (as if I would be judged by an implacable god of honesty; turned away at heaven's gates, never to see or feel or know what might happen next).

Eventually, we stopped playing truth or dare: we grew out of it, I suppose, even though it had grown into us in ways we did not realize then. I was probably about ten when the game faded; the same age as my younger son is now. (Halfway through writing this piece, I asked him if he still played truth or dare, and he looked surprised – not because he didn't know about the game, but because I did. 'How come you found out about it?' he said, unable to disguise his disbelief, as astonished as I would have been as a child if my mother had told me that she, too, had played truth or dare with her brothers, once upon a time.)

But it was my sister's death, a decade after Simon's, that made the telling of truth seem so necessary again;

about the past and the present and how I had come to this hard place, and how I might move on. It was not that I'd been living a lie until then, though in adult life we may decide, for all kinds of good reasons, that some things are unsayable. 'Better left unsaid': that's the theory, anyway, except now the truth felt visceral, vital and alive and far more than a diversionary pastime, in the way that the game itself had been *not just a game* when we were children. Simon died when I was still at Cambridge; he had been at Oxford, but was killed in a climbing accident in South Africa – the country where our parents had first met as university students themselves, long before marriage and children. This was the place of Simon's birth, as well as his death, almost as if he had completed a full circle long before he should have done; not that it seemed like a circle to me then, nor a zero, nor any kind of symbol at all, but something wordless, a shadowy horror which could not be fashioned into a meaningful shape.

Simon was a year older than me, and had occupied a very particular role in my life – all of my life – which was a curious mix of fraternal and romantic. I had never known his father, who died in a plane crash when Simon was still a little boy, but his mother was one of my mother's closest friends, which made it seem as though we were almost part of each other's family (close enough for our first kiss, beneath the blankets on his bottom bunk, to have felt forbidden). He was tall and fair and clever and handsome, and he took risks, too, in a way that I did not; or at least, different kinds of risks to me, though as teenagers we were both still caught up in those reckless leaps, that seemed to be moments of freedom, but might have been something else. I chose difficult, dangerous boyfriends – as if daring myself, as if daring Simon to declare himself – and he climbed mountains. 'Why?' I asked him, one Christmas, when we had come home to my mother's house for the holidays.

'Because of that split second of uncertainty,' he said, 'when your hand slips and there is no ground beneath your feet.'

When he died, I felt he was not mine to grieve – he was his mother's son, and her loss was unimaginable, terrible and savage and hers alone; so it was not for me to say that I missed him, it was not my place to speak of him, his story was not mine to tell. After Simon, other friends died – close friends, my own age, too young, not peacefully – but it was his ghost that came to life for me again when my sister died. And it was as if the two of them had been reunited in a final round of the game – both of them in a high place, ready to leap, or perhaps already soaring free, leaving me behind.

And there was nothing for me to do but try to tell the truth; no other way to attempt to survive (just as my sister – my fierce and irrepressible sister – had written about what it felt like to have terminal cancer, refusing to go quietly, calling out to the world as she contemplated the silence of the dead). This was the voice I heard inside my head as I wrote a memoir that charted the search I made for my sister, and for myself, after her death. 'Truth or dare', it whispered, 'Dare to tell the truth.'

The trouble is, in trying to write the truth, it can turn into something else. (And truth, for me, was inextricably linked with Ruth, as a word as well as an idea: for to be truthful was also to be full of Ruth, and in this attempt at capturing the truth of what it meant to lose her, I was also bringing her back to life.) Anyone who has told a story knows how the chaos and messiness of life can be shaped into a neater narrative, with a beginning and a middle and an end; the rough edges of misery, rage, fear or confusion, chiselled away to make a joke or a sonnet or some other form of wordplay; the choking lump in your throat transformed into fluency. And as I continued to work on the book, I wondered, too, about my claim on the past; a past that in resurrecting I was also remodelling, because my memory was not – could not be – the same as anyone else's; my story was not my parents' version of events, nor my husband's, nor my children's. Searching, late at night, for a guide in the thicket of confusion (for this was a wasteland without a map; uncharted territory, to be newly navigated each day, even as the days turned into months), I found a passage in Jacques Lacan's preface to *The Four Fundamental Concepts of Psycho-Analysis*: 'All I can do is tell the truth. No, that isn't so – I have missed it. There is no truth that, in passing through awareness, does not lie. But one runs after it all the same.'

On the whole, I was finding Lacan as impenetrable a guide as everything else at the time. But those words seemed marvellously clear to me, unlike the murmurs of my ghosts.

Since *If The Spirit Moves You* was published, I have heard other people's stories: in letters and emails from strangers; in the middle of parties or at the edges of a crowded room. It's as if in telling my tale – an ordinary one, that speaks of the grief and loss that is part of being human – I have also become a listener to those others who want to share their spirits with me. And I always listen carefully, for these are the stories that cannot be ignored, and every

Introduction

narrative is different, and yet also the same, as well. There are few constants in life, but they underpin our stories: we are born, and we love, and we die.

Of course, a ghost is not the only secret waiting to be discovered: there are joys, as well as sorrows, that refuse to be silenced; memory reveals itself in a myriad of ways, with quiet, fleeting moments holding their own against more apparently dramatic scenes. As the stories in this collection begin to make clear, there are as many different forms of truth-telling as there are tales to be told: an infinite number, as wide and as deep as the sky, limitless and without boundary, like the place I imagine my sister and Simon to be.

It is no coincidence that the initial idea for *Truth or Dare* (this book, that is, rather than the game, which must be older than the words attributed to Jesus by St John in the New Testament, that 'the truth will make you free') chased around in my head while I was on a quest for my sister. And as you might expect, there are various other journeys and searches undertaken within these pages. Nick Hornby, for example, writes about learning to drive so he can take his son Danny, who is autistic, to the places they need to go; his piece is as swift and deft as an escape to freedom, at the same time as containing within it the idea of capture and endings. The idea of escape is also alive in Andrea

Ashworth's passage across the desert, as well as an exploration of what might constitute happiness (and how it both eludes and possesses us). Elsewhere in the anthology, there are expeditions into the past, discovering the unknowns hidden within the familiar; odysseys to Blackpool and Lapland and Las Vegas.

But what all these writers share is the courage to take that leap: to try to express that which is closest to their hearts. It is an act of bravery on the part of a writer, to say, yes, this is how it is; this is who I am; this is what it means to be me. Some of them have already explored similar landscapes in fiction – because a novel can be an act of daring, too, that goes hand in hand with autobiography, performing a similar duet or double-act to that childhood game we most of us have played. So there may well be resonances to be found here, for anyone who has read Esther Freud's novels, or those of several others who have contributed to this collection. (I'm not suggesting that readers should become literary detectives, searching for clues and mirrored writing – but even so, someone who has loved, say, the happy ending of Sabine Durrant's first novel may feel it to be a precious, hard-won victory, having read her memoir.)

For all that, these pieces can be read without any other context, taken simply for what they are: as

Introduction

voices that speak with a rare candour and openness, whether telling of first love or of rape; birth or death or the arc of a life, glimpsed and held and let free. But I don't want to say any more – it would be giving the game away. Truth or dare – which one will you choose?

Open Sky
Andrea Ashworth

Through the dunes the road zooms like a spool of thread forever unravelling. We're speeding across the southern Californian desert, the needle's tickling up to a hundred an hour, but there's a gorgeous air of stillness here inside the car. We're the only souls in sight: with an engine so big and smooth, the sun shimmering off a sandscape that's naked and never-changing, it's as if Mark and I are just sitting here, floating, the last – or the very first – two people in the world.

A cool, air-conditioned breeze is whispering across my bare feet, propped up on the dashboard. I've penned faces on my big toes and I flex them now and then, Miss Eyelashki and Mister Moustachio, doing puppet theatre for myself and Mark, who's behind the wheel. He has to do all the driving, since I still don't know how. Usually, I pretend to be useful by wafting the map, balancing coffee and preposterously stuffed sandwiches, but we haven't seen any signs of civilization, or even quasi-civilization, for miles – and miles and miles and miles.

I switch on the radio and, without any twiddling or tuning, it pours out Bach, rich and strong.

'*Nice*,' Mark says, the back of his neck softening. The cello suite's one we listen to over and over at home.

'Home,' I hear myself murmur.

My toes freeze. Where is home, exactly? My chest goes tight and stringy, tied up with the gorgeous complexities of the music and the delicious but elusive idea of belonging, feeling settled.

I rub my bare heels together and turn, excited, to Mark. 'Won't it be great when we have our own place?' My heart lifts itself by leaping forward in time, as it has always done, since I was little. 'Our very own home?'

'Yeah.' Mark smiles. Then his brows scrunch. 'But we already have two great homes, don't we?'

Snug in the middle of Oxford, we share a warren of medieval, half-timbered rooms. And a gorgeously light-filled, blonde parquet-floored apartment is where we live when we're in Washington, D.C., not far from where Mark's from. I love both places, but endlessly shuttling between them, as we do, can be exhausting. I tend to wander around, catatonic, end-of-the-worldy when it's time to catch a plane, clutching a spaghetti-strap sandal in one hand, finally discovering its equally unwearable twin in the freezer, next to the ice cream.

Mark takes his eyes off the road to glance at me. He's distracted, unhappy to find me anything less than happy with the way we're already living. This boy, this man, does everything, although he makes it seem like an airy nothing, to make my life sweet.

'We *do* have two lovely homes.' My toes agree, nodding sagely. 'It's just that, *for me*, two's too many. Two add up to *less* than one, you know?'

Mark looks from Miss Eyelashki and Mister Moustachio to my face. 'Yup,' he says, in a voice warm with respect for my heart's own mathematics.

Two hours have melted under the sun since we left Las Vegas, an almighty pinball machine, spitting and popping, catapulting us out in our silver rental car. After flying in from London, we had piled straight into a car to start driving east, away from the neon. I'd felt anxious, wanting to explore Vegas right away. I still didn't quite believe in its existence – or in my own existence, in the playground of a life so bright. But we had decided we would definitely go back, after our desert sojourn, to stay in Caesar's Palace or some other

Open Sky

Christmas cake of a hotel, on our way home to D.C., then England.

Mark had hugged me, hard. 'We're gonna go wherever you like.'

We met, Mark and I, two and a half years ago at Jesus College in Oxford, where I held a junior research fellowship in English literature and he held one in philosophy. After being awarded the JRF, I'd felt so grateful and excited, I kept zinging out of bed to daze around Oxford in the misty dawn; I could not sleep for days. I still laugh, remembering my even more profound and breathless discombobulation after moving into college, when I realized I'd got blessedly more than I had bargained for: the three-year prize of holding the junior research *fellowship* was one thing; the possibly lifetime prize of holding this darkly handsome junior research *fellow* was something else. We've spent hardly any time apart since we first dined together two and a half years ago at High Table, in our bat-winged gowns, chatting, shy yet effusive, amid the candelabra and ancient oil paintings and comically demoralized broccoli. Older fellows, with beards and clever, kind eyes, ploughed more sedately through their meat and potatoes and smiled over their spectacles at us.

After dinner, Mark and I would lie on my futon under the ancient eaves and whisper about music and science and movies and books and family and food and philosophy and faraway countries we wanted to discover. 'Together,' Mark said. And our nights are still full of loving and whispering and staying up way too late, wired with questions about the world and what makes it tick, in small ways as well as big, and ideas about how we are going to make a good life on its soil.

I rest my head against the car window and close my eyes and the optimistic cinema inside the lids calms me.

When I open my eyes, I fall back into the trance of the unending road and Mark's calmness and my faith in him and myself. My toes pick up their waltz.

'We do have great homes. *Homes* . . .' I start playing with, truly relishing, the plural, '*Homes-ZA!* As many homes as we like. Wherever we are . . . Like right here, in this car.'

I tease up the radio's volume. Bach whirls like divine, shimmery blankets about us, cosy and glorious, both at once.

*

Open Sky

Where we're going is invisible to us. The road keeps unfurling and then dissolving, unfurling, dissolving, before it ever touches the horizon. The horizon: it flirts like a silvery streak of tinsel, somewhere forever far off, in the future.

'Mum would adore this,' I say to Mark. 'Driving and driving, as if we might never stop. Might just keep on going, forever . . .'

I tell him how, sometimes, in the middle of the night, when we were kids, Mum would come shrieking upstairs, fiery-eyed, to drag my little sisters and me out of bed and bundle us, in our nighties and anoraks, into the back of the car. To get away from my stepfather's fists. Or, other times, awful in their own under-the-skin way, we'd be slowly peeled out of bed, half asleep, when my stepfather was gone and the house was silent. Silent, but not calm.

Those nights, Mum needed to get away from fists in her heart.

'Where are we going?' Sarah would ask, sleepily, afraid.

'Away.' Mum would grit her teeth. 'Away.'

There were swishy, winding roads, arched over with great grandmotherly trees, that my mother found, on the posh side of Manchester, curling into the country-side. We'd speed through them in the pitch dark. A frightening, delicious darkness pierced only by the orange fizzle of her cigarettes, which she'd suck raspingly, fast, fast, angry and fast, lighting a new one just before the old one burned out, as if to keep her temper alight. As if, when the cigarettes and the anger expired, so might her heart.

Lindsey and Sarah would cuddle quietly on the back seat, dazed, wordlessly slipping, lulled by the hum of the engine, back to sleep. And I'd sit in the front passenger seat, the seat of honour, listening to Mum's tearful rants and offering small, grown-up-sounding consolations. Or just holding my breath in the midst of one of her salty, oceanic silences.

The road's curves loomed, sharp, in the dark. But Mum drove smooth, smooth, smooth, as well as heart-squeezingly fast.

The trees rushed by, a foresty blur.

How could anyone not think of crashing into their trunks?

Finally, after ages and ages flying along the road, imagining we must have crossed over some magical edge and finally escaped from Manchester, I'd hear the gears grind and shift, mellowing down.

Then Mum would turn the car around, to head, snakingly, back home.

Her cigarette would flicker slowly out, while it was

still long and ripe, and she'd put it to rest in the packet. Whispering, bitter-sweet, 'For tomorrow.'

Suddenly, here in the baking desert, our sunshine's blotted out. A host of tiny smacks on the windshield reminds Mark and me that we're not floating, but shooting forwards at bug-splatting speed.

'Ugh! *Creatures!*' I pull a face at the rain of gloopy insect innards. 'Can't you use the wipers? Wash them off?'

But there they are, sticking, in spite of the wipers' shrugs. So many tiny wings pinned, some still wriggling. The dead and half-dead creatures aren't just disgusting; they make me feel guilty. If we weren't shooting through their space, they'd be fine, buzzing about their own business.

At the same time, I'm a touch thrilled: all that invisible life in the air. Coming at us, out of nowhere. It's as if they're throwing themselves at us, wanting to splat, spectacular, to be part of our speed. I can't help thinking of my mum and stepdad.

'Kamikaze romantics,' I say.

There are so many that, once we're through the dark-winged cloud, we have to stop and scrape the jammy splurge off the windscreen, so we can see where we're going.

'Phew! Maybe April *is* the cruellest month.' I wipe tears of sweat from my face.

It's barely springtime, but already the desert's a furnace. Getting back into the car is like diving into a cool swimming pool. I reach for the bottle of water, but it's all gone. Mark reckons, in a mysterious man-and-map way, that we'll come across some place for food and drink before long.

We zoom and zoom and mountains loom. Vast, stoic, bald rocks, with no foliage to hide all their cranial lumps and bumps. Instead of making them featureless, this seems to show up their personalities. To me, a lot of them look the way most babies are said to look, like Winston Churchill. But, see, there's a demurely gorgeous Audrey Hepburn, and there's an extravagantly undulating, wittily cragged Oscar Wilde and, for Mark, I find Mohammed Ali, Babe Ruth and a colossal huddle of other baseball and basketball heroes. We wrangle over one particular magnificence, which flirts like Marilyn Monroe, but turns out, when we drive closer, to be the obese old Brando.

We're busy naming the mountains, with their grumpy brows or sublime noses and their creeping five o'clock shadows, when night falls.

Just like that.

I lower the window and feel the tang of night air. The desert has let go of its heat with a single sigh of darkness.

JACKASS AEROPARK. PAHRUMP JUNCTION. The signs are flatulent poems. There's no evidence of habitation, but for a few spindly wood and metal constructions here and there, doleful orthodontics on the landscape. I wonder if anyone lives in any of these places?

'People can live anywhere,' Mark says, in a voice that takes in the sadness and triumph of this truth. 'People are amazing.' He squeezes my knee.

Finally: lights by the side of the road.

A sign says *AREA 51*.

'Area 51?' I shiver, and do the *Twilight Zone* tune, '*Da-da-doo-doo, Da-da-doo-doo . . .*'

We pull up to a shack festooned in red lights. NEVADA JOE'S.

'This looks good,' we agree. A weird but cheery kind of place. Maybe they'll be serving some deep-fried South Western chicken and spicy greens and mashed potatoes. Or a gigantic steak. With a mountain of fries. We've been fantasizing feasts for more than a hundred miles.

But, closer up, it seems the main thing on Nevada

Joe's menu is aliens. They're glowing in the dark, painted on the outside walls. And, once we push through the door into the fluorescence of what turns out to be a twenty-four-hour fast-food store, we're met by more and more extraterrestrials, all neon green with lovely-horrible, oversized eyes and no proper noses or fingers. Alien dolls, alien T-shirts, alien caps and sunglasses, endless UFO and alien candies.

Mark's shoulders lose their oomph in the face of no simple, old-fashioned, down-to-earth food. I, meanwhile, am in heaven. I pick up a moon-eyed Martian with silver antennae that are straws. 'For Hannah,' I say. Hannah's the beautiful, spirited little daughter of my sister Sarah. My baby sister Sarah, who was always *my* beautiful, spirited little girl; my sisters let me mother them throughout our childhood in a way that helped save me from my own fears.

Mark smiles. He knows our small niece will love the bottle; and he knows I'll love 'looking after it' for a while, along with all the other silly nothings I collect before posting them to her in London. My heart fluffs and I feel small, physically, when I pick up candy or a book or a toy for Hannah – as if *I'm* the child getting the treat. Then, when I wrap up the present and put stamps on the package, I feel taller again, grown-up.

'*Gotta* eat.' Mark sticks his hands in his pockets and

his shoulders hunch, concrete, as he quests off down one of the bright, plasticky aisles.

We find doughnuts like meteorites, covered in green gloop and technicolour sprinkles. We find Twinkies, those spongey torpedoes filled with jam and sweet, sweet cream, which give you a nasty-fantastic, almost electrical jolt of energy, then knock you, just as suddenly, comatose. And we find masses and masses of jerky – beef and pork and chicken and ostrich and alligator jerky. Long, skinny sticks of shrivelled flesh.

'O . . . K . . .' I raise my eyebrows and move on, while Mark lingers in front of the jerky, straining to adjust his dreams of steak, to shrink his appetite to fit what's here.

'I'll work out the highest prime number before I eat this stuff,' I whisper.

I wander up and down every aisle, then approach the extremely bearded, thin-necked, Jesus-resembling man at the cash register.

'Excuse me,' I clear my throat and try not to sound like Holly Golightly, 'do you have any bananas?'

Several guys, eyes hidden under the brims of heavy-looking cowboy hats, turn to inspect me from a less well-lit corner of the store, where, it dawns on me, they're taking their nice old time to choose X-rated videos. My words, so English and silly and wondering about bananas, are still ricocheting off the fluorescent-lit walls.

'Or water?' I ask, more quietly, keen to seem less odd – among the aliens and cowboys.

'Or *what*?' The pale, bearded guy perks up, intrigued.

'Water?' I repeat, tentatively. 'Do you have any sparkling water?'

The man's bony fingers crawl into his beard, as if he's looking for something.

'Or, you know, just plain water?' I add, smiling. 'Without bubbles.'

The man is shaking his head, looking paler.

I'm beginning to believe that they just don't have water, when Mark emerges from the meaty reeds of jerky to come to my rescue. 'Water,' he says. '*Wawww-derrr*.'

'A-hah!' The man's fingers spring from his beard, and he jerks his thumb towards a refrigerator.

I imagine dying of thirst because nobody here understands me. Here, *I'm* the alien. I see the headline: *Englishwoman killed by own accent*.

I find the refrigerator just past the fleshy videos, next to a door covered with a dark red curtain. As I'm grabbing bottles of water, the door opens with a limp tinkle of bells and a gaunt woman, dressed – which is to say, not very dressed – as a bunny, rushes into the store and grabs a Twinkie. She tears through the plastic wrapper, takes a vicious bite, then relaxes and holds up the oozing sponge to salute the guy at the cash register, 'Thanks, Hank!'

Then she disappears back behind the dark red curtain. Where the real, twenty-four-hours-a-day business of Nevada Joe's is going on. The big, bouncing rhythms of Dolly Parton flirt out from the brothel's bar.

'Only in America.' Mark blinks and shakes his head, as we pull out of Area 51, as if from a dream.

I'm the proud owner of a UFO made of neon pink and blue ice cream and, for 'real food', we have a stash of pretzels and liquorice and water. Also several packets of dried ostrich and alligator rump, to which we seem to have grown attached – as if they're pets.

I look back over my shoulder, giggling. 'Only in America.'

Through the car window, the night air breathes in, vast, as I sip icy water through my Martian's antennae.

NOWHERE ELSE IN America, or the world, is there a college like Deep Springs, just west of the Sierra Nevada mountains. That's where we're going to be staying for the next month or so, while Mark teaches philosophy to some of the two dozen students, who have a whole valley to themselves; their tiny, autonomous college is pretty much the only thing there, but for vultures and sand and sky, sky, sky.

When we finally arrive, after midnight, the place is hushed and dark. The purply-black heavens are lush with a startling embroidery of stars.

In the kitchen, we find a few boys with bird-nesty hair laughing over an industrial-sized frying pan, sizzling up some massive, mysterious treat.

'Hey there.' They offer us a share of their psychedelic omelette.

'It looks nice.' I eye the eggy confusion, spotted with lumps of meaty this and mushroomy that. 'But I'm OK, thanks.'

'OK, later.' The boys retreat into the darkness with their Unidentified Fried Object.

We saw thick slices from a home-made loaf of bread to make toast. It smells scrumptious; it smells of home. Mark, Americanly, shovels mounds of peanut butter onto his, while I, Englishly, slather mine in profoundly yellow, creamy butter. 'Courtesy of Gertrude the Cow', it says, in felt-tip, on the butter tub. The same words are scrawled on the jug from which Mark pours two frothy glasses of milk.

'To Gertrude.' He clinks his glass with mine.

Open Sky

He knows how much I adore fresh, whole milk. Knows what heebie-jeebies I get from that anaemic, skimmed stuff that reminds me of powdered milk, which was often all Mum could afford when we were kids. It's not just that it tastes dismal; it's that having to drink thin, soul-sapping milk or instant coffee, or feeling cold inside the house, or running out of toothpaste or toilet paper – all these things give me subtle but strong shudders. They yank me back through time, make me afraid I'm about to be expelled from this nice life, to be sent back to the scary corners of my childhood. I know, in my head, that it's silly. But sometimes my heart cramps and I feel afraid that my escape from the past is temporary, provisional. That this life with Mark is not real, but only a holiday: soon the bell will ring and I'll have to go home.

'How about that?' Mark turns off the electric light and we sit with our hot toast and cool milk at a table sploshed celestially bright.

'Mmm . . .' I whisper, 'Where's that light coming from?'

We go outside and marvel at the voluptuous disc, so vivid, unveiled by clouds.

'Moon milk!' I stick out my fingers to splash in the silvery-white beams. We sit down to finish our toast on the steps outside.

Instead of the candelabra we're used to at High Table in Oxford, there's a tall, skinny cactus watching over us, a Giacometti loner, lit up by the moon.

I kiss Mark in this otherworldly light. 'Thank you.'

Next morning, the sun rises to reveal the intense, time-seared beauty all around.

'Wow!' My eyes are aching with the sight of the mountains, too awesome to take in. I laugh because my contact lenses keep shrivelling and pinging loose, as if my eyes are falling out of my head. Mark explains it's because the air's so dry. We're 5,000 feet above sea level. That accounts for the slight ache niggling my temples, like a grumpy crown.

Mark cracks ice-cubes out of their tray and they swirl into my glass and I love the plinky, playful music they make.

I knock back the water, not sure which feels more delicious, the cool, cool liquid streaming down my throat, rinsing and trickling to soothe my head, or the coals that glow in my chest when Mark reminds me, as a mother might, to take care of myself.

*

Open Sky

In the yard, bare-chested boys come and go, talking of Michelangelo.

At the same time, they're lifting and shifting, heaving machinery and timber, helping to build a new classroom for themselves. Each student labours for twenty hours a week on the farm or on the ranch or in the kitchen, having received a full scholarship for two years' tuition from professors they hand-pick for themselves. After that, the boys transfer to Harvard or Cornell or some other prestigious school to finish their degrees. Then they tend to go off and become men who'll do something terribly heroic or more subtly useful with their analytical passions and earthy, globally attuned intellects. Architects, environmental developers, altruistic lawyers, doctors, professors, writers, musicians – they often shape their lives around Renaissance-man combinations of professional and creative pursuits.

This place strikes me as a cross between a Wild West ad for Levi jeans and a nerdy brain farm, spiritually sponsored by Emerson and Henry David Thoreau, dedicated to churning out perfect young males. Guys who can cook and clean and do dishes, who can wrestle cattle *and* appreciate Proust. Every last, everlasting sentence of Proust: these boys go way beyond the epiphany on page eighteen of *Swann's Way*, I soon discover. Me, I've never ventured beyond that moment where the madeleine sponge is dipped in tea and all the memories whoosh up, so you're in another world. Whether you like it or not.

Days start at half-past four in the morning, in the dairy, where three of the tallest, jolly-giant boys hunker down on tiny stools to milkmaidenly commune with the cows and their udders. Everyone else gets up a couple of hours later to start studying. Around nine, classes begin and they unfold with more and more intensity, so boys are often still clustered in talk when lunch wafts its savoury fragrances at noon. Seeing them, I get goosebumps, remembering how excited I was when I went to Oxford and found myself surrounded by people who wanted to gossip about books and plays and pictures; friends with whom I spent years sharing ideas and Jaffa Cakes and Hob Nobs. A darker memory shadows the first. Christmas and Easter holidays in rainy, grey Manchester: having to disguise my enthusiasms and hide my books. My stepfather hated the sight of them; if he caught us with books and papers, he'd fly into a rage, grabbing them and hurling them down into the cellar.

After a rich lunch, the Deep Springers are all bare

feet and loose spines: a frisbee flies desultorily across the central circle of grass, lanky boys stoop to play ball with the farmer's small children. Then it's time for physical labour, cooking and building and tending the alfalfa fields. After tea, there's hiking or reading or napping under the sun until dinner is unveiled just after six.

Every evening, the sunset's an apocalyptic aperitif. People stop what they're doing and just stare at the great star on fire. Radiating violent pinks and oranges, sliding down the shadowy sky. I try to describe it to my mother in a letter. I wish she could have a sunset, every night, like this, crushing time in its fist. Promising a heavenly fresh start, day after day.

After dusk comes dinner. All of us, twenty-four boys and about a dozen men and women – professors, office staff, the farmer and ranch manager – gather together to enjoy masses of food prepared by the boys, under the aegis of a professional chef. Succulent chicken, home-bred sausage, garlicky spaghetti, spinach, beans, tofu, bread that's perfectly dense and perfectly fluffy and hot, slathered in that fantastic butter, courtesy of Gertrude.

'Mm! Amazing!' I keep exclaiming from behind my mountainous plate.

Then I blush, realizing I seem, in my effusiveness, the most sexist person here. Knocked sideways by the deliciousness of everything, all this lovely stuff put together with nary a female finger lifted. There are women here, a couple of professors and some omni-competent, super-hearted office ladies who make everything tick, but they don't do anything when it comes to the food, except eat it.

'Your favourite,' Mark says, coming back from the buffet counter with two huge bowls of apple crumble, steaming sweet and tart.

'*Yeah.*' I only wish there were some custard, or ice cream.

A beautiful boy, with purple mascara-tickled eye-lashes and auburny hair longer than mine, reads my mind. 'Oh, oh, oh.' He flutters his pretty hands and runs to the kitchen and totters back in his slingback heels with an ice cream scoop and a massive tub labelled CLARISSA.

I feel like a child, an adored child, sitting there with my hot apple crumble and oodles of surreally fresh ice cream, whose flavour makes me wish I could invent a better word, one with many more syllables, for vanilla.

'Clarissanilla.' I christen it, and the farmer's three blonde cheruby children screech laughter and clang their spoons on the table and chant, 'Clah-wissanilla! Clah-wissanilla!'

*

Over the weeks, Mark and I get to know the boys, who are sweet and serious and funny. Each one sports idio-syncratically whimsical hair, sculpted by sandy winds, dyed blue or pink, plaited in long pigtails or chopped off in some capricious inspiration in the night. Each boy's clearly happy to be himself and at the same time curious, keen to play around with his identity, working on and playing with his mind and his heart, in ways that are colourfully adventurous without being shrilly insistent. As the weeks pass, each boy seems a little different. It's like watching a time-lapse film of flowers blossoming, witnessing these boys growing into themselves. Tall, short, skinny or beefy, they all share a kind of confidence that seems to me magical.

In this valley, they're protected from the world. At the same time, in this valley, they've made a world. A family.

I feel guilty, I tell Mark one night, living so happily among strangers, people who aren't what my mother would call 'blood'.

'Some of the happiest families,' Mark gloops minty toothpaste over his brush, 'aren't related by blood.'

I confess the urge I used to suffer, until very recently: wanting to adopt other people's parents. I used to meet grown-ups, or even just see them, in shops, or on the bus, and imagine slipping into their pockets, going home to live safely, nice and quietly, with them. It gave me pain, because it seemed impossible. But mostly it hurt because it made me feel guilty about my mum, whom I love, love, love, but could never associate with the cosy, emotional umbrella I imagined a 'real' family offering.

Of course it's too late, now I'm on the way to being thirty, for me to be adopted into anyone else's family.

'Stupid, stupid,' I chide myself aloud, still trying to shake off the old urge. 'Too late.'

'Ott are oo 'alking a'out?' Mark widens his brown eyes at me in the mirror, his toothbrush samba-ing back and forth. 'E're 'amily, aren't 'ee? 'Oo and 'ee?'

I giggle and shuffle closer to him. Pressing, warm, so that the muscles of his strong arm send ripples of energy into my spindlier one, inspiring my toothbrush to dance over my teeth in tune with his.

Our bedroom is the only residential room at the back of the large institutional building of classrooms.

Mark had regretted, when we arrived, that we could-n't stay in one of the idyllic cottages in the valley, because they're being renovated. 'I wanted something nicer for you.' He had kissed my neck apologetically. 'This feels kinda tacked on. Superfluous.'

'I like it,' I had assured him. 'It's not superfluous, it's . . . improvised.'

And it's true: I love the idea that we've made our own den behind the classrooms. I like the fact that it's not a 'real' home, but we can make it so, just by being in it. Each morning Mark sets our little espresso pot on the stove and it burps like a belligerent frog, then yields up smooth, dark coffee, to which he adds great splashes of hot milk, the way I love it. Each afternoon we hike and I stop and stop again to find the most perfect wildflowers and stones with quirky personalities, to arrange in the middle of our small table. At night we play Bach or the Rolling Stones on my tinny portable cassette player and slip into bed with thimble glasses of whisky.

And on the bed there's a fresh lemony quilt. Each night as I huddle under it, I know that I'm going to have lovely, meringuey dreams.

And most nights I do have lovely, meringuey dreams.

Other nights I'm running through the dark house. The roof is crumbling and so is the floor, but I see a way out, there is a way out, I can see blue sky. I have to stay inside, though, in the hot shadows, to find my sisters, my little sisters. My mother is running about and screaming. Her hair's on fire. Her hair's on fire, but I can't scream and

I just keep holding my breath and swimming through the fiery silence, looking for my little sisters.

Sometimes I find them. There they are: girls with the pretty faces and sweet-smelling hair that I love. We're outside, in a field, running about in the gentle sun, like the girls in *Little House on the Prairie*.

But sometimes I don't find them.

My mother's hair keeps burning and when I get close and reach out to help her, *Mum! Mummy!* she runs away, wailing, 'Leave me alone! Leave me alone!'

As if her crown of flames is a precious, beautiful hairdo I'm threatening to spoil.

Ay-eeeeeeeeeeeeeh! Ay-eeeeeeh! Ayeeeeeeeeeeeeeeh. The fire alarm screeches through the bones of our building in the middle of the night. Emergency lights are flashing, white, white, stabbing bright, *get-out* white. The alarm keeps shrieking. *Ay-eeeeeeeeeeeeeh! Ay-eeeeeeeh! Ayeeeeeeeeeeeeeh!*

The noise and lights claw Mark and me by our throats, ripping us out of sleep. Our heads are exploding.

The world is exploding.

'*What . . . ?*' Mark leaps out of bed, straight into his

clothes. His eyes are a bad dark. I've never, before, seen fear in his face.

I lie there. Spineless.

The unearthly noise and lights have spiked into my dream and mixed everything up and yanked me way back in time.

'I can't move,' I say, pinned, suffocating, under the quilt. 'Can't.'

Mark has to dress me as if I'm a doll, sticking my feet into my boots, my arms into my coat, before half carrying me down the apocalypse-flashing corridors and out, out, out into the icy night air, away from the explosion of lights and blasting sirens.

We hustle across the sand, then, finally, stop and look back.

No flames.

No danger. Just an electrical blip.

I'm laughing and crying and still half paralysed. Not just by exhaustion. Not just by the fierce frost biting into our faces. But by a refusal, a tearful and angry refusal to keep running when I'm ripped out of sleep into a shrieking universe.

'I don't *want* to run any more,' I cry petulantly, sticking out my bottom lip like an eight-year-old. 'I just wanna go back to bed.'

Mark strokes my hair and sits me down next to our

favourite, soulful cowboy cactus, while he goes to get someone to shut off the sirens and lights.

I can't go with him. I can't let anyone see my face, etched with tears and old fear, crowded with ghosts.

I sit there shivering, naked under my thin coat. Remembering.

All those times: sprinting down the road in the dark in my pyjamas, to fetch a policeman to come and save Mum and Dad. From themselves. I scrunch my toes, sockless inside my boots, and can't help thinking of my little sisters' feet, which would get slashed up when they were the ones that ran while I tried to keep Dad and Mum apart. I might get clobbered in the eye of my parents' storm, all the words and fists flying, but my sisters would come back from the police station with their soles bloodily shredded, stones and bits of broken glass sticking out. When I screamed 'Run!' they would run. They didn't stop to put on their shoes.

Not like me, sometimes deciding to sleep in my shoes.

Not like me, ever ready with a plastic bag stashed under the bed: clean knickers and socks, a spare toothbrush and a book, a few Bensons' blackcurrant and liquorice sweets for luxury, and any bits of change I might have managed to squirrel away.

I take off my boots and settle my bare feet on the cold, sandy ground. The moonlight shows up the little

knobbles I have on the bridges of my feet, from perpet-
ually wearing heavy boots, ever since I was sixteen.
Boots in which I could always run if I had to, boots that
helped give me ballast. I'd wear them with everything
and anything. I wore them under my gown when I went
to the ball, ten years ago, at Oxford.

Midsummer night; I'd just turned nineteen. My girlfriends were frothing about in their gowns, all the pink
and green and blue silks, and the boys were stapled into
tuxedos, their hair heartbreakingly neat. The night was
cold but I felt warm as I dashed about in my flimsy, charity shop confection of a frock, which I'd stitched and
mended that afternoon, after spending the morning
cleaning toilets and kitchens in North Oxford houses,
earning money for fun things and for books, books,
books, which, like bricks, made safe, beautiful walls
around me.

'I *love* your dress!' Even the poshest girls, the ones
with real pearls, paused to admire the black sweetheart
bodice and the fairytale skirt, a poof of pale lilac silk,
adorned in tiny black velvet fleurs-de-lys.

Passing from one music-and-light-and-laughter-filled
marquee to another, I tripped over a huge iron peg
lurking in the ground in the dark. It tore my dress and
gashed my shin, deep.

'O my God! O my God!' Everyone fussed when they

saw the blood. One girl bent over, as if she might throw up.

And the gash throbbed like a monster and I felt sea-stormily sick and it was clear the wound was going to leave a scar. But it didn't, in the real sense, hurt. My friends mopped me up and brought me champagne and rich, squishy-centred chocolates and, though the cut was nasty, I could keep my heartbeat in place.

'It's only an accident,' I kept saying. 'I'm fine. I'm really fine.'

'I can't believe you're not crying,' a Christ Church girl said, her pale hand clasped across her freckly chest. 'Are you sure you're OK?'

But the friends closest to me knew why, truly, I did feel fine, in spite of the gash. They knew I came from a childhood of bloody accidents that weren't accidents – unless you considered them accidents of fate.

IN A WHIRL of teaching, writing, reading, talking, hiking, time shines by under Deep Springs' big, bluest-blue sky. Happiness and confidence are silting up inside me, moment upon moment, luxurious.

One incredibly bright afternoon in the yard, I watch the farmer's youngest daughter playing in the sand with half a dozen gnarly yellow and orange gourds. She places the gourds around her, in a circle, like wobbly acolytes. 'Wah-on . . . Two-ooh . . . Thur-ree . . .' She starts out frowning, slowly positioning her gourds. 'For-orr . . .' She shifts them about. 'Fy-ive . . .' They fall down and she has to keep uprighting them, so she forgets where she is in her counting. 'Thur-ree . . . *no!*'

'No,' she repeats, quietly, to herself, then starts again, placing the gourds in a passionate, imperfect circle. 'Wah-on . . . Two-ooh . . .'

The sun diamonds off her white-blonde hair. I think of my youngest, blue-eyed sister, Sarah, who was also white-blonde as a small child, dreamy but stubborn, like this little girl. Only born under a darker sky. In spite of all the wrongs done to her, my baby sister has grown up to be astonishingly successful, not only in her field of cardiac technology and physics, but also as the mother of a beautiful little girl, Hannah, who lives in her own charmed circle of security and confidence, far away in London.

'Six!' The farmer's daughter claps her hands, triumphant. She sits in the dust, a princess, surrounded by six gourds, each bowed worshipfully towards her.

*

'Idyllic,' I find myself scribbling on postcards to friends, wishing I could share some of the magic of these days with them.

Then, one afternoon, the single, collective telephone rings. And, when the secretary comes to get me and I pick up the receiver, there is my mother's smoky-sweet voice: 'Andy, love?'

'Mum?' I'm so happy to hear her, I almost say, *Mummy?*

But, in the middle of its fluttering, my heart suddenly shrivels up. Plummets.

I have nausea in my knees: there's no way, it strikes me, that my mum would be calling across all that ocean and land, all the way from Devon to Deep Springs, at British Telecom's 'hib – *bloody* – larious' prices, unless something was wrong. Drastically wrong.

'Is everything OK?' I ask, trying not to sound shaky. I wish there were another, more private, phone for me to use. The line's crackly, so I can't whisper, the way I'd like to. I feel suddenly anxious to keep my concerned daughter self separate from my effervescent desert self. A few of the people here know I've written a book about my childhood; they understand that my past is story-worthy in some scary and sad ways. And I don't mind people knowing, as long as they don't feel sorry for me – which nobody, thank goodness, seems to feel when they read the book and then look at me, knowing.

But, somehow, this phone call, its real, live, here-and-nowness, makes me shy. Also a touch panicky, confused. I so often cruise through my life believing, almost, that my childhood was just a weird story – only distantly, abstractly, related to my life now.

Mum's throat is a clutch of wild elastic bands. 'It's Derek,' she says, tightly, too quiet.

I ask, gently, 'Is he OK?'

Mum's partner of five years has been seriously ill. His bones are riddled with arthritis and he's recently suffered a stroke, although, like her, he's very young, not even fifty years old.

'He's *sick*,' Mum says vehemently.

'I know,' I say. 'But I thought he'd got a lot better?'

Derek had, it emerged, been stoking his illness, which started out mild and run-of-the-mill, by refusing to take his pills. Mum believes he brought on his own stroke, in a bid to keep her at home. Her paid job is to go out and tend to other people, physically and mentally handicapped young people, who are often violent towards themselves and their carers. But Derek wanted her to stay at home and be *his* nurse. His alone.

O God; I know this story. I've seen men trying to

stamp their signatures on my mother before. On her face, so often coloured with bruises. On her body, sometimes using their boots, kicking into her bare flesh.

But no man has ever made himself ill, on purpose, as a way to control Mum. This gives me the iciest creeps. Like the time my stepfather smashed the teapot into his own temple and the spout cracked off and blood dribbled down his face, in place of tears.

My sisters and Mark and I have just gone through a horrible winter, feeling frightened for Derek's life, worrying that the paralysis that followed the stroke would never go away. But then, just before Mark and I headed out West, Mum had devoted more time to being at home and mobility had come back to Derek's body in a miraculous rush, his collapsed face bouncing back to normal.

'Yes, Derek got bloody better,' Mum's hissing. 'He's completely better. But he's *sick*.'

Oh, I see: *sick*. Mum has seen into the soul of her partner and she's disgusted and afraid and has run away to live in an extremely small room above someone's barn.

'It's great that you're in a place of your own, Mum.' I grasp for a silver lining, as I always do. It's an emotional tic. Give me a mad, melancholy elephant of a cloud and I'll wrestle forth a ludicrously sparkly lining. But I'm also genuinely relieved that my mother has, at last, left this man, after so many months and years of dreaming but never daring.

Mum takes my point, but she bloody well *does* not think it's great. All her furniture and clothes are still back in the house she lived in with him, and he's refusing to let her have what's hers and so, OK, fine, stuff it, let the bugger have it all; what does she need, anyway? God knows, she's survived with nothing, less than nothing, before.

But – something's snapped in Derek. Something, something.

'I don't know . . . I don't know . . .' She takes hefty puffs on her cigarette.

Now Derek's coming after her all the time, stalking her day and night, night and day, chasing her, trying to run her down in his car.

'I had to get rid of my Mazda,' Mum says, mournfully.

'What do you mean?' I remember, I *felt* her pride in her little white, nearly new car, all her own, for which she lovingly slaved, even going without cigarettes to save money. I'd bought her a new angel – she loves angels with a passion that's almost fierce – to dangle from the rear-view mirror.

'I thought you adored that car, Mum. What happened?'

Mum explains how she was sick of having Derek chasing her everywhere in her white Mazda, so she got up before dawn one morning and sped to a car dealer and traded in her white car for a blue car. A shitty, rusted thing, she sighs, which breaks down all the time. Especially in the middle of roundabouts. Especially during rush hour.

'But why did you trade in your beautiful white car for a rubbishy jalopy?'

I still don't get it.

'So Derek would stop following me *in the white car*,' Mum reiterates, as if I'm stupid.

And I do feel stupid. I despair of understanding her actions, sometimes. My mother is an intelligent, feisty woman, a woman with a lot of nerve and wisdom, a head as strong as her heart. An amazing woman. But here, horns locked with her bloke, caught in what my sister Lindsey, who lives in Paris, so beautifully calls a *'rapport de force'*, she's gone and thrown her brain away with her beloved car.

'But – doesn't he follow you in the blue car?' I stick doggedly to logic.

Mum pauses.

She admits that, within four hours of her acquiring

the blue car, Derek was back on her tail. Now she has to hiccup up and down the steep, serpentine roads of Devon in an old tin can on wheels, getting nowhere fast, with a madman hot on her heels.

I think of Sisyphus. *Sisyphus*: such a nice, sybilant name, for such a sad, cursed soul, condemned to go heaving his rock up the hill forever, never quite reaching the top, always rolling down, back down, in an absurd, never-ending struggle.

Beckett sings in my blood: *You must go on, I can't go on, I'll go on*.

I feel guilty for consoling myself with little twists of myth and irony and art, airy-fairy, like candy. Or vitamins. My secret fortifications.

'Oh, Mum.' I bite back tears.

'But I *did* piss him off!' she says, and I hear her taking a victory puff on her cigarette.

Then I have to laugh, just for a second, appreciating her triumph at foiling the enemy. Throwing him off, if only for a few hours.

But the line crackles and Mum's voice fades as she sinks back into her feverish fret.

'Wouldn't it be better if you just, you know, ignored him?' I suggest. I think of Derek, a small man with a mousy voice, who has never raised a finger to hurt my mother in all these years. 'Even though,' Mum has often paused to give him this major credit, 'he *knows* what those others did to me. No, even though he knows what they did, he would *never* do it to me himself. He's a good man.'

I remind Mum of all this, trying to reassure her – and myself.

'Well, that's the Derek *you* know,' Mum sourly enlightens me. 'But that's *not* the Derek I'm dealing with now, believe you me.' She quietens. She seems truly, deeply afraid. She adds, 'He's got a gun.'

The line is hissing and fizzing. I could've sworn she said 'gun'.

'He's got a what?' I ask, in front of everyone in the office. All the ladies are trying to busy themselves making coffee and chatting, to weave a cocoon of discretion around me.

My mum's intimate, number-one enemy has a gun, it turns out, a gun he uses to shoot rabbits.

'Derek shoots rabbits?' I'm stunned. 'Are you sure?'

Oh, yes, Mum has seen him shoot rabbits; she's gone out hunting with him, plenty of times, on the Devonshire moors.

My forehead's dripping sweat.

'You haven't shot any rabbits, have you?' I whisper.

I can't help asking. Suddenly I need to know that my mother has never shot a rabbit.

'Course not!' Mum snaps. 'What would *I* be doing, shooting rabbits?'

I laugh weakly, feeling unhappy, but relieved. Mum, got up like Elmer Fudd, aiming a rifle at bunnies – with that picture crumpled away, the world feels more manageable.

I also feel safer nowadays than I used to when Mum was in a mess with a man, knowing I have someone to turn to, someone who will understand and won't panic and will know what to do.

'Don't worry.' I assume the mumsy voice I often slip into with my beloved, beleaguered mother, 'I'll talk to Mark.'

Mark is a lawyer as well as a philosopher and an extremely calm, sensible person, who also happens to have big muscles and a very deep voice. How this combination of qualities can do any good across six thousand miles, I'm not sure. But it makes me feel better.

'I'll talk to Mark,' I say, as soothingly as I can, 'and we'll work something out, OK?'

California's eight hours behind England, so it's too late to do anything to help Mum today. I smile at Mark. I try to bury my nose in a book. But the pages won't let me in. My nerves are fizzing. I stand up. I sit down. I stand up.

I put on the coffee pot, feel a flutter of optimism, with the scent of espresso, then switch off the gas in a blue-black huff. I've burned two fingers on my right hand.

'It's OK,' I say, when Mark rushes to apply ice.

'It's gonna blister.' He tuts, at once caressing and indignant, quietly but strongly indignant, at the way my past can rear up and get me.

We look together at the burn. I say, 'I know.'

I go to lie down on our lemony quilt. I do a dead-man float, staring at the ceiling.

After a while Mark comes and leans in the doorway.

'Wanna go for a ride?' He throws the car keys to me.

I catch them, niftily, with my left hand and, in catching them like that, I feel suddenly lucky. Confident. Enough to break out of my dead-man torpor and sit up.

'Yup.' I smile my lop-sided smile. 'It feels like a good moment.'

My flip-flop, with its gold-sequinned butterfly, is lightly pressed to the gas pedal. I can feel the heart of the car, ready to roar.

'Whoa!' I blush, embarrassed at the power lurking beneath the butterfly and my toes.

We take off and I laugh hysterically. 'Feel the G forces!'

This is my first driving lesson, ever. The speedometer's skulking just under twenty miles an hour. Down the mud road, massive balls of dried grass and dust go bowling along like ghostly buffalo. Overtaking me.

I look at Mark and he's looking at me in that impressively (sometimes infuriatingly) patient way he has. His face resting in neutral gear.

'Just do it your way.'

No pressure. Also, no idea what he's thinking.

I put my foot down.

The engine leaps.

I let it go. *Go, go, go.* It's revving up to thirty miles an hour. I dare a glance over at Mark: 'Look at me!'

He's smiling. The more I press on the gas, the more he smiles. Happy to see me taking off. Around fifty miles an hour, his smile goes into reverse: the more I press on the gas, the more his smile shrinks. But it doesn't give up.

I suffer a big surge of love for him.

Then I decide that fifty's a bit much for me, and

panic to put on the brake. My flip-flop's confused: I hit the gas and we jerk forward into a crowd of shrubs.

'Oops!' I look sheepishly at Mark. His patience seems indefatigable.

I look at my butterfly flip-flops. Mutter, 'Right is accelerator. Left is brake.'

And so it goes, me flirting with forty miles an hour, then fifty, shooting forwards, edging backwards, Mark crooning, 'Good . . . Great . . . Nice,' as we shimmy down an empty mud track in the middle of nowhere.

This is Mark, patient and gentle. Only when it comes to Truth does he heat up. That's the one real argument we've ever had: about truth and relativism. I'm a soppy relativist, always comparing and contrasting circumstances and perspectives, explaining certain people's actions in terms of the particular, often invisible pressures on them. Perhaps, as a way of rationalizing my mother's actions, I've come to believe in different flavours of truth – in a rainbow of fine calibrations, defying the black and white of right and wrong. Mark sees and appreciates that people live in different ways and look at life from different angles, but he doesn't believe in a plurality of meaningful individual truths. He believes in bigger, shared truths. He believes in Truth. When we argued about this, in Manhattan, over frozen margaritas, I burst into tears and

Mark was bewildered. There he was, discussing truth as a philosopher. And there I was, dressing up in an armour of literature and physics and art, but all the while, in my own way, defending my mother. To myself.

Through the rearview mirror, I see something glinting in the dust in the distance. I do a rococo three-point-turn, and then speed up, up, up, to sixty, spitting sand, drawn towards the glinting thing.

Mark puts one hand on the dashboard in front of him. His arm stiffens. He puts his other hand on the dashboard, and that arm stiffens too.

I conjure a slow, controlled stop, smooth as molasses.

'Nice,' he says, his arms loosening. He tries to hide the fact that he's very glad to get out of the car.

Shimmering in front of us is, of all things, a boat. A small, wooden boat with a rusty propeller engine, washed up in the middle of the desert. Inside the boat sits a TV. A huge, wide-screened monster, obviously new and very fancy. And smack in the middle of the screen is a bullet hole: someone has blown the machine's brains out.

'They could've just changed the channel,' I quip.

Deep down, I feel spooked. All the hours my family and I spent, clustered around the altar of our fizzing

TV, tensely worshipping. Killing time. Straining to be a family.

Mark stands in front of the massacred television and the stranded boat. Mesmerized.

The sun begins to set, inspiring the screen to glow, orangey-pink.

'So beautiful,' I whisper.

I feel tearful. Suddenly full of hours, all the hours of my childhood. Full of my mother.

If I cry now, Mark will hold me.

But if I cry now, I'm not sure I'll ever stop crying.

'Shall we go?' I tinkle the keys, and he says, 'Sure.'

On the way back, I go slow. Nice and slow, nice and careful. Still, the car weebles, left and right, like a disobedient supermarket trolley, as if it's mad at me. Has ideas of its own. The bumper scrapes against shrubs and then the car judders and I stall, rudely, against a rock.

'Three-point turn,' I say to myself.

But I'm too darned tired.

I think of my mum, stalling at roundabouts. A man with a gun just over her shoulder.

My throat stings, salty with unwept anger. How can it be? How can it be allowed? How were my stepfathers allowed to threaten us, all those years, with carving

knives and pans of boiling water and letter bombs?
Why did nobody do anything about it?

I glare at the rock in my path.

'Do you mind if I really *do* do my own thing?' I ask
Mark, who shrugs, 'Whatever you want.'

I get out of the car, ready to heave the stupid stone
out of the way. Enough with this game. I have no intention of trying to cha-cha-cha around this one, thank
you very much. 'Rules, schmules,' I say to myself as I
bend down, incredibly angry at the stone, '*Fuck you.*'

My own words surprise me. After a childhood
whose air was pumped full of fuck and bloody and bas-
tard, I almost never swear. Our house was riddled with
dramatically double standards, which back then
seemed sharply unfair, but actually helped save my sisters and me from more dismal futures. Mum chivvied
us to mind our *p*s and *q*s and she strictly forbade us
from swearing; even calling one another a pig or a cow
won us immediate, disproportionate punishment.

'*Fuckfuckfuck*,' I'm muttering, when I see something
that gives me a jolt.

I wave, excited, to Mark, 'Come see! Come see!'

And then I kiss him, because, for once, although
he's a boy with a face so often parked in neutral and a
mind stuck in cloudy abstractions, he *sees*.

Blooming across the rock, in the last of the sunlight, is an exquisite veil of lichen. Its surreal, blood-orangey colour is *exactly* the same as the colour of the psychedelic, seventies bikini I'm wearing.

I get back into the car, feeling comforted. Connected. Energized. As though someone, someone, has reached out to tickle me with a surreal little hello.

That night we huddle around a fire with the boys and toast marshmallows and try to tell ghost stories, but end up laughing and arguing about Plato and Socrates and personal identity and free will, all the things firing up the students in Mark's class. When Mark and I go home to our room for whisky and bed, we have to candle our way through the dark corridors, because a storm miles off in the mountains has robbed Deep Springs of electricity.

There's no Rolling Stones, no Pergolesi, no Bach cello, none of the usual lullaby tracks from my tinny portable cassette player. No sounds, but for the whispering night winds, which press, imploringly, against the windows.

'Mum,' I sigh. She'll just now be getting up to start another day, far away, in a world that is all hard work and bloody worries. I can practically hear the click and whoosh of her little gold lighter, the soft crackle of the cigarette she'll be kissing, slowly, thinking, or trying not to think, as she wakes up.

I know that, in spite of tonight's laughter and hot marshmallows and this balmy quilt and the cradle of Mark's arms around me now, I'm in danger of stumbling into a bad dream. But I'm not worrying, not really, I assure Mark, as he strokes my hair and I go melting into creamy sleep, because I know it will be only a dream.

There is a man. A man with a gun.

But it's not Derek. Who is it?

'Andy,' the man whispers. And then I see. It's my stepfather, my second stepfather. I haven't seen him since – since he almost strangled my mother.

'Andy, love.' His blue eyes are twinkling and I love him, I do still love him, with a fierceness that hurts, even though it's crazy, after everything.

'Da—' I begin to say Dad.

Then he shoots me and my chest explodes.

A bright orange bloody flower.

I wake up aching all through my body, with flu, and with a fierce, cramped-muscle desire to hear my mum's voice. But all the lines are down: no telephone, no fax, no email. For three nights and days an incredible storm takes over the valley, making everything gloom. We may as well be in outer space. There's no way to find out if Mum's OK. No way to let her know we're thinking of her.

'Are you breathing properly?' Mark checks on me between his classes.

Sometimes – but only sometimes, nowadays – my chest clams up and I can't breathe, except in short, hard gasps that rip my throat and make my head spin. Hyperventilation, it's called. Practically everyone in Mark's family is a doctor and he's very down-to-earth, unmystical, about such things. He grabs a paper bag when the suffocation thing happens and asks me to breathe in and out of the bag. 'Breathe, breathe,' he repeats. I listen to the stern nursery rhyme and I obey it. And after a while the spinning, bad-starry feeling goes away.

But now the bad spinning persists, for hours, in my feverish head.

The sky churns, a dark spill of sour milk, and the winds come whistling and whipping. Brave desert shrubs dance maniacally and cling to their sandy moorings like skinny ladies with disastrous perms. I look through the window at the shrubs and feel so sorry for them it hurts. I have to close the blinds, so I can't see them.

Then, on Monday morning, there's a lull. Stillness, and a shaft of sunlight.

Mark borrows a cell phone from the college president. He sets off to climb a nearby mountain. He has 'a few ideas', he says, about what to do to make things better for Mum. At the top of this particular mountain, it's rumoured, you can sometimes achieve a smidgen of contact with the outside world. You have to find just the right spot, you have to stand just so. And you have to be lucky.

In spite of the heavens, the FedEx man turns up at the end of the week, hungry and thirsty, having trucked over four hours through beautiful nothingness just to make this one stop.

'Weather's a killer,' he says cheerily. He has to make the same long haul back through the storm to the depot, and that will have been his whole day.

He's brought something important for me to sign. A mortgage-related document, covered in a rash of small print that makes no sense to me except that I know it will ensure that my mother can finally have her very own roof. Mark and I have urged Mum to find a place of her own, we've set the financial clockwork in motion, and Mum has, with her usual, desperately flamboyant resourcefulness, discovered a wonderful place with tall and wide windows, through which she can see and hear and *smell* the ocean. This will, Mark and I hope, protect her from mad, bad or dangerous-to-know men – much more powerfully than any legal injunctions.

'I'm so sorry.' I offer the FedEx man coffee and apple crumble and profuse apologies along with dollops of ice cream, thinking he's come all this way just for me. Just for me and my mum.

'No-ooo sweat.' He knocks back coffee and digs his fork into the steaming apple crumble. 'This time the pleasure *surely* was all mine.'

He's had company. Strapped to the front seat: a box full of fluffy new life.

'Just cheepin' and cheepin', so I couldn't hardly hear all the rain!' He hands the box over to the boys, who gently lower it to the floor and kneel around it.

Mark and I kneel down, too. I gasp when the lid is lifted. Crackles of delight come off Mark's skin; the hairs are dancing on tiptoe along his arms.

Inside the box, a hundred tiny creatures are shuffling about, lemon bonbons with hiccuppy wings.

'Elektra!' 'Tess!' 'Bathsheba!' 'Cleo!' Everyone calls out glorious girl names.

'Optimissima,' I offer a name, under my breath.

And the first chick comes hopping out of the box, squawking and shivering, right into Mark's palm.

There's easy, sweet sadness in the hugs we exchange when it's time to leave Deep Springs.

'Shame you couldn't stay longer.' People commiserate with us for having to leave earlier than we'd planned.

'Hope your ma feels bedda soon.' The farmer smiles. I've told people my mother's unwell, physically.

I have to get back to her as soon as I can. To sort things out, and just be with her. We've changed our flights and we're going to drive to Vegas today, so tomorrow we can fly straight to England and I'll be with my mum.

I kiss people goodbye and feel full of them and the time we've shared. It's weird, feeling warm and good about a goodbye. Not empty, peeled and hollowed out, the way I can't help feeling when it's time to say goodbye to my mum. As if she might not wait around for me to come back to see her again. Might decide to 'disappear', rather than put up with the pain of waiting for me to come back. I suspect she frets, secretly, that I might just not come back.

'*Thank you*,' she often exclaims, out of the blue, in the middle of a conversation about anything and nothing, 'Thank you for still being here, Andy. Loving me.'

'Oh, Mumsy!' I squeeze her bony, soft-skinned hand. 'Course I love you!'

'I don't deserve it. I know I don't deserve it.' That's Mum's searing mantra.

'Don't be silly, Mum!' That's mine. My heart breaks in the face of her anxieties, but I smile and croon my bossy lullaby: 'We love you. We *love* you. And that's that.'

I kiss her hand, then kiss it again and again, and then I make another nice, strong cup of tea, to help drown some of her ghosts.

BEFORE HITTING THE straight, long highway to Vegas, we have to broach a narrower, nausea-jogging road that swerves wildly through the mountains. I feel squiffy when we stop to use a telephone in the nearest town. The good news is that Mark and I have spoken to Derek and Derek has, under the stereo influences of my wheedling cop and Mark's inscrutable cop, agreed to put a peaceful, unmelodramatic end to what he calls 'all this confusion'. Now I'm calling to check he's sticking to his promise.

'I don't know how it all got so crazy . . .' Derek muses in a small, faraway, almost helpless-sounding voice. 'How did everything get so out of hand?'

My face burns. 'Well, I'm glad it's all over now,' I say, delicately.

'I love your mother,' Derek keeps insisting in his oozy voice. 'I'd never hurt her, would I? I'd as soon hurt meself. I adore your mother, Andy. I adore her. You know that.'

'Yes,' I say, because it's the right, peace-keeping thing to say.

And, it's true, I do know that – about the adoring. And I hope I'll never be adored like that in my life.

Mark's arms stick out, stiff, the veins protruding, unhappy blue, as he drives. The car jerks over bumps; wordlessly, he shifts gears.

I itch to keep the question down, but eventually it pops out of my mouth: 'You're mad at me, aren't you?'

Mark hates it when I ask him that. We both know it's a hangover from my childhood. He's rarely mad at me, and when he is, there's no hiding it. His forehead scrunches into deep, deep, wavery lines of disgruntled calligraphy.

Still, there are times when I can't help asking Mark whether he's mad at me.

I get a chilling, nails-on-chalkboard rush down my back, for no reason I can decipher: I'm in trouble, my bones tell me, though I don't know what for. I don't know what I've done to deserve to be punished. I just know I'm in trouble and someone is going to hurt me. Sometimes it happens at parties and I feel too hot, trapped inside my dress, jailed behind my own face, which just keeps on smiling.

I think Mark believes it's hormonal, this fear of mine, though he has never, to his credit, voiced this suspicion. To me, the fear feels bigger than hormones. Vastly beyond me.

When the fear comes, like now, I *have* to ask: 'Are you mad at me?'

'No,' Mark sighs. 'Just tired.'

My spine's itching with guilt at taking him away early from Deep Springs. I'm ashamed of all the anxiety and trouble I've brought into his life. It's not the first time I've been unable to sleep or stop crying because of my family. And, although this crisis is abating, it's unlikely to be the last.

'You *are* mad at me,' I say, in a small voice, hoping

he's not. 'Your forehead's doing that thingummy' – I squiggle my fingers across my own forehead – 'with the lines.'

Mark laughs and it steams the crinkles out of his brow. His arms relax and he reaches to switch on the radio. I get ready to feel relieved. To feel cosy and happy.

But what seeps out of the speakers is vinegary guitar and blunt-tonsilled wailing. Mark twiddles the knob, hitting on hollow rock and roll and more evisceratingly forlorn country and a lot of God-hollerin' sillivangelist stuff. He grunts and kills the radio and we cruise in silence.

After a while, I say, in an officious, very English voice, 'I think you *are* mad at me and you just won't admit it.'

Even as I'm saying it, I realize these are my stepfather's words: the accusations he used to use on me, when I was little. Always trying to get me to admit that I hated him, so he could slide off his belt and give me a good whipping.

Mark looks at me, his eyes warm, then returns his gaze to the road.

I fold my arms tight across my chest and sink deeper into my huff.

The sun rises with a modest, hesitant blush of bluey-yellow.

Within minutes, it's burning, wild gold, across the sky. Mark grins.

I don't smile back. I think I want to. But I can't.

Several silent miles slither by, then, 'Whoa,' Mark says, peering out across the salty, white sand. 'Is that water?'

He stops the car and gets out to size up this oasis in the middle of stark dry nothing. A wide pool of water, crystal clear, with a shallow bottom of golden sand.

'*Wow!*' He pulls off his T-shirt. 'Wanna come in with me?'

I gaze at the oasis. The water's twinkling, as if it holds some marvellous secret, under the sun.

I look up at Mark, from my seat in the car. 'Are you . . . ?'

'Sure.' He grins. 'It looks so cool.'

'No,' I say, exasperated. 'Are you . . . *you know?*'

Mark glances to the heavens. 'I'm *not* mad at you,' he says, 'but I do think you're a bit mad. Come on, get out of the car and take a dip with me, huh?'

He finishes taking off his clothes and he looks heart-stoppingly beautiful. His strong body glowing in the morning sun, as if he's lit up from inside, electric cream pulsing through his arteries.

My mother's words fill my head: *I don't deserve it, I*

know I don't deserve it. I look at Mark and imagine leaving him, making him free to be with someone else, someone who hasn't been where I've been, hasn't seen what I've seen. Someone unsullied. Pure.

'Coming?' He beckons from the edge of the pool.

I want to get out of the car and laugh out of my clothes and slip into the cool, clear water with him.

But I'm stuck in here, in the car, in my sulk. I stay fastened under my seatbelt. I put my hand up and press my fingertips against the window, and stare, dazed, where the sun lights up the bones and the veins.

I'm gazing at my hand, a self-pitying starfish, when Mark vanishes. One moment he's standing there, dipping his toes into the shallow pool. The next moment, he's gone.

Just like that.

A weird trick of the light. The desert is full of these illusions; it loves to play games with your eyes.

I unclick my seatbelt and lean forward to peer through the windscreen.

He's really gone.

There is the pool. But where is Mark?

I think I hear his voice.

I jump out of the car and dash to the pool.

There is Mark, up to his nose in angry yellow slime.

'Quicksand!' I start unbuttoning my shirt, though I know that plunging in will only double our trouble. I jump up and down, helplessly, at the edge. 'Marky!' I hiccup out the nickname his brothers used to use on him. He hates it, but it makes me feel better to say it, 'Marky. Marky.'

'Jeez!' Mark breathes, once he's hauled himself out of the pool. No gentle, shallow oasis, but a deep, infernal sludge of ancient sand and the fermenting mud of dead creatures and plants.

I rush to kiss him, but gag: my stomach heaves at the stench. His skin is covered in mustardy primordial vomit, reeking of sulphur, warty with sinister, gritty blobs dredged up from the desert's guts. I bend over and, as soon as the nausea's subsided, I move towards him again. Still, it's impossible to embrace him. He's radioactively yellow, covered in the earth's worst ooze. And he stinks, so badly, my eyes water.

Mark looks a bit stunned. I can't tell how he's feeling.

Next to him, I feel tinglingly clean and fresh. Pure.

'You don't smell so good,' I say, uncertainly.

'Tell me about it.' He wipes his feet on sparse tufts of papery grass and sticks them back into his sneakers. Apart from his sneakers and the cloak of ooze, he's completely naked.

Before long, the slime has baked onto Mark's skin and he can crack it to dislodge it. He stretches and bends, inspiring flakes of subterranean crust to fall off.

'You're hatching,' I laugh, 'like a chick!' I look at his nakedness, and add, 'With a few – differences.'

I try not to show him that I'm holding my breath. Strain not to inhale the miasma off his skin.

Out of the corner of my eye, I inspect him. He looks cute and a bit frightening. A yellowish ghost. After a while, he glances at me.

'Hey.' He raises a mischievous eyebrow, loosening foul, mustardy flakes. 'Are you – *mad* at me?'

I laugh so hard that my eyes, stinging from the sulphurous air, weep.

In a cavernous room, dimly lit and clouded with the fumes of Marlboros and cheap, sausagey cigars, goddesses are hovering in torturous headdresses and skimpy togas, which urge leathery cleavages up towards their chins. I cringe at their poor heels, stuffed into stilettos while they walk mile after smoky, shadowy, indoor mile every night, here on the bottom floor of Caesar's Palace. And there's me, wandering around in my desert-dusted jeans and flip-flops and my white old-man shirt, all rumpled up.

'How do you suppose it feels,' I whisper to Mark, 'being paid to be diaphanous?'

'I'm not,' Mark deadpans, the way he responds whenever I ask him something girly, 'the right person to ask.' Although he spent more than half an hour in the shower, lathering through two mini-Acropolis columns of soap, his skin's still offering slight whiffs of swamp.

We wander through the abysmal, bilious-carpeted fields of the slot machines, one-arm bandits whizzing cherries and lemons and hearts, hollowly clanging and ker-chinging under a low, low ceiling flashing migrainey neon. An old lady buzzes past us on her white scooter, clutching, with the one, single arm she possesses, an obese tub of quarters conjured with almighty 'don't-mess-with-me' patience in the face of the spinning machines. From an oxygen tank in the scooter's front basket, wires curly-wurly out, their ends stuffed up the lady's nose.

Escaping into the world of roulette wheels and green baize tables, we find the ceiling is blessedly higher, though sinisterly dotted with a galaxy of cameras and spy holes. It might be one in the morning, it might be two or three, or nearly dawn; I've lost track. There are no clocks and no windows, no slices of sky to guess time by. The goddess who gives me a Martini doesn't wish me a nice day. Out of the side of her mouth, she drawls, 'Have a nice . . . *whaddevva.*'

In a low-scooped gown, a woman bows her svelte, tanned back over the cards of her swish-shirted guy. My eye pounces on the sparkle of her real diamonds, then leaps to the next lady's goluptiously fake gems. The crap tables look like little ships, glamorous passengers clinging to the sides, hollering and groaning, hoping to stay afloat. Or perhaps hoping, in their own shadowy ways, not to stay afloat.

Around the quieter card tables, the whole world is huddled, elbow to silent elbow. As in a crowded but sludgy dream. Laconic cowboys and tired dentists and thirsty secretaries and patient plumbers and stoical nurses and whisky-wired granddads and many, many lost-looking, hapless-haired grannies, all alone, shorn of their outlived, beloved or not-so-lovely husbands.

I look at all these people and, suddenly, I know them. That frightening feeling: I *am* them. Could be them. Could have been.

I take a sip of my Martini, but find it's sour.

Mark puts his arm around me. 'Tired?'

'Yeah,' I admit, 'I'm tired.'

*

On the way back to our room, I pass a gift shop noisy with fur coats and crocodile handbags and diamond jewellery that lets you take home a spangle of Vegas in your ears or around your neck. The price tags are mind-boggling. But the white, tight-faced wives stroking the furs, casually deciding whether to adopt one, don't pause to finger the tags. They are interested in money, in costly things, but they aren't interested in how much things cost.

When I walk in in my scruffy shirt and unwashed jeans, rolled up at the bottom like a farm girl's, I feel the older women looking at me. I catch a lady inspecting, it seems, my muddied butterfly flip-flops. When I smile at her, tentatively, she looks me sharply, half admiringly, in the eye. As if to say, *I hope you know what those ankles of yours are worth? I hope you're making the most of them.*

I feel my spine lengthening, quietly proud. I feel free to stroke the furs, wildly soft and alive-smelling, though I have no desire to own one.

At the jewellery counter, my eyes land on a tiny angel. A delicate diamond brooch, with a halo that sticks out at an endearing right angle from the small round head. Faceless but benign, modest and wise and wry. A surge of desire washes over me: this angel looks *so* lucky; I want to get it for my mother, though it's sure to cost a mad wallop of money.

I pick it up, drink in its sparkle, then turn it over, braced for the price. But it's less than twenty dollars: it's diamanté.

'May I take this, please?' I lay the angel on the counter.

The assiduously blonde shop assistant is a warmly chatty lady called Gala and she is from the Ukraine and I can see that she forgives the audacious modesty of my purchase because she likes my accent. 'Sounding like Prrreensess Dee! But ze eyes.' She looks warmly into my face. 'Zese eyes neeser than Prrreensess Dee. Making you better prrreensess, ov yourr own: Prrreensess You.'

I laugh and blush and tell her I like her eyes, too. They're striking: sharp, icy white-blue, but warm.

'Nees, verry nees,' Gala holds up the tiny angel, then swathes it in pink tissue. 'You want bow?' Her plastic talons flick through a box of silky gift bows. 'I find one gold, for you.'

'Thank you. It's for my mother,' I tell her. 'She loves angels.'

'She is lucky lady,' says Gala, 'daurrrter like you, loving her.'

'I'm the lucky one.' I blush at this flutter of intimacy

with a stranger – a woman about my mother's age. 'I'm a very lucky person,' I tell her. 'Much luckier than my mother.'

'I see you lucky.' Gala's long, press-on nails pause among the tissue and bows while she contemplates me. 'Lucky wis zese eyes. Zis hair. Good air all about. And nees boy somewhere?'

I nod. I can see Mark waiting outside in the plush, red-carpeted corridor. He hates shops; they make him itch. His head's bowed over a piece of yellow paper, crumpled from his back pocket, trying to decipher some of his own mad-spidery notes.

'Lots of things lucky,' Gala says to me gently. 'But life not so simple always. Zis we know. But your mother, I say she is lucky. And zis enjel bring her more luck and more. You vill see.'

In spite of the angel glittering in pink tissue in my pocket, I feel raw, unsparkly, as we head up to our sumptuous room. I'll be with my mother within a day or two. But my excitement's dampened by dread about how she'll be when I see her. The man trouble is over, for now. But I'm afraid of the trouble Mum can bring on herself, the way she can hurt herself, keep herself down, when there's no man there to do the punishing.

At the window of our room, Mark and I stand close and drink in the ripple and clash of Vegas's wild, all-colourful lights.

'A strange kind of beautiful.' I press my face against the glass. The window's designed never to open more than a few inches. So nobody can leap out. 'Don't you think it's beautiful? In its own way?'

Mark looks. Lights whirl and flash, reflected from the crazed world outside into his large, dark eyes.

'I like the desert,' he says. 'Peace.'

A woman's voice stabs through the wall, jabbing me out of sleep.

My neck prickles as I lie there, pinned to my pillow, trying to tell whether she's laughing or crying. I listen and listen and can't work it out. After a while, her eruptions simmer down into something gentler, giggles or tears. I lie wide-eyed, wondering. Tears or giggles? Giggles or tears?

In the dark, I feel frightened. I wish Mark were awake.

The sheets have slipped down the bed, revealing

his back, smooth as dunes. It rises and falls, peaceful. Radiating warmth.

I blow into his ear, but he doesn't stir, so I stroke his shoulder.

I lean over to press his nose, firmly, as if it were a doorbell.

Then I give up and lie back down, sighing.

It's the sigh that awakens him. He rolls over and his eyes open, big and lost. His pupils focus slightly and he says, sleepily, 'Hey.'

'Hi.' I prop myself up on one elbow and look at him quizzically, expectantly, as if he's the one who's just woken me.

'Have you been crying?' He frowns.

'No.' Then I taste tears that have dribbled down my cheeks to my mouth. I lick my lips. 'Maybe.'

'Light?' He likes to cast brightness across the night when I wake up out of a dream, shaken. Like a splash of cold water, it brings me back to myself. My here and now self.

'OK.'

He clicks on the light and I snuggle into his chest. After a while, I turn around, to be a little spoon, basking in the heat of Mark's body and the sunny glow from the bedside lamp.

'I like it when we make our own secret daytimes,

like this,' I murmur, deeply calmed, 'in the middle of the night.'

Then, 'Oorgh!' I jolt up off the pillow. It's streaked, I now see, with dried blood.

'Ow!' Mark rubs his chin, which I've whacked in my haste. I rub the crown of my head, where it collided with his chin.

'Oorgh, oorgh.' I rush to the bathroom to wash my face, which has been lying in the dark on a pillow streaked with the blood of a stranger. '*Oorgh!*'

I start concocting baroque, death-in-the-afternoon scenarios, to go with the streak.

Mark is anti-dramatic about it; to him, it looks like nothing.

'Probably just some guy cut himself shaving,' he conjectures, ready to fall back to sleep. 'I'll call house-keeping for fresh pillowcases.'

'It's *too late* for fresh pillowcases,' I moan. 'I feel sick.' Adrenaline's swirling, spouting and trickling, inside me.

I sit on the edge of the bathtub, letting its porcelain coolness seep through my skin, to my bones. I take a few deep breaths. Still, the walls come closing in.

My jeans are lying, moulted, on the bathroom tiles. I think of my angel – my mother's angel. All its tiny, lucky sparkles.

But when I reach for it, inside my jeans' pocket, there's nothing there.

'Have you seen my mother's angel?' I call to Mark from the marble bathroom.

'Your mother?' he responds drowsily.

'*No*, my mother's . . . never mind.' I start sifting through all the clutter I've generated across the bathroom. Everywhere I go, I spray a bit of chaos: glittery hairclips and books and papers, lollipops and chocolate and knickers and whimsically patterned socks that make me look as if I've been lobotomized, or ought to be. As kids, Mum made us keep our house – or whatever spare room our friends and family let us stay in when we were homeless – extremely clean and tidy. Excruciatingly so. Desperate to please her, we once asphyxiated her beloved rubber plant: spraying each leaf with Mr Pledge, then polishing and polishing, lovingly, to make the thing *gleam*. Clean is in my blood. No getting away from it. But tidy has, spectacularly, kicked out and escaped me.

I whirl through the room, stirring my chaos about, making everything worse, looking for the sparkly angel. I look and look. I fail and fail to find it.

My poor mother. I sit back down on the edge of the bath, devastated. Poor Mum – her angel gone. All the luck sparkling in its wings and its halo. Gone.

Open Sky

Saltiness comes chasing up my throat, heading for my eyes. But I don't want to cry. I've cried so much over my mum. Nights I've wept so long and violently, I've been disconcerted, truly thrown, in the morning, to find that my eyes are still dark, dark brown, that the colour's not all washed away.

'I'm going,' I say, huffily, to myself. To the tears.

I grab knickers and unmatching socks out of my bag and yank them on. Green and gold seahorses on my left foot; the right foot red and furry. I stumble, hustling into my jeans, and hit my head again, against the wall. From the bedside drawer, I grab my wallet and *Moby Dick* and the remains of my chocolate toffee crunch bar. Lip balm, toothbrush, passport.

'Where are my eyelash curlers?'

'Eyelash curlers?' Mark slides out of bed, bleary-eyed. 'Why do you want eyelash curlers? We need to sleep.'

'I'm going,' I say.

'Where?'

'Away.' I find my eyelash curlers and start crimping my lashes, stubbornly, in the mirror. 'Away.'

Although I've had only a few hours of sleep, it's already way past dawn. I march down the corridor to the elevator, where a wide window offers a vista of Vegas under the morning sun. I look out across the confusion of electric lights, competing with sunshine, at the pyramids and Sphinx, the Eiffel Tower, a massive pirate ship, a gigantic wizard and so many lasers wiffling about, streaking the awakening sky.

My eye lands on the Stratosphere.

Like a child's, my heart jumps.

I turn around and go back to get Mark.

The Stratosphere is the tallest tower in Las Vegas, about two hundred feet high, and at the top of it a needle sticks up – another twenty or thirty feet – into the air. For a small sum of money, they're going to allow me to attach myself to the outside of this needle and get blasted towards the heavens. At a force of 4Gs.

'You're sure you don't want to do it?' I ask Mark, once we're at the top of the tower.

'Believe me.' He crimps his lips. He has no fondness for heights. It's the one dimension in which I feel braver than him.

First thing in the morning. I'm the only person to climb up to the needle.

I take my seat and am shocked to find I'm just sitting there, outdoors, at the top of the world, nothing between me and the vastness of sky.

'Is this it?' I ask the man in charge of the ride.

Open Sky

There are no straps or belts on my seat. Just two metal arms over my shoulders, padded with rubber, so I don't bruise.

The man nods. 'You go, girl,' he says, kindly. A bit grimly.

Down on the lower platform, a crowd of tourists is gathering, looking up. Some of the people are grinning; others are, plainly, horrified. I search among the faces for Mark. On the edge of the small crowd, standing a shade to the left of everyone else, he's there. His face in neutral. *Just do it your way.* I wave shyly at him, and he widens his eyes a touch.

Then the needle buzzes, releasing a profound, almost religious hum up my spine.

Before I know it, my body is in the heavens. My hair flies out, long, dark, wild, around me. My stomach has fallen behind, somewhere dozens of feet below. Also my lungs – I seem to have misplaced them, like a handbag at a party.

I can't breathe. I can't breathe.

But I can see the whole world.

My brain's imploded and sherberted down to my toes, which are tingling. It takes all my strength to draw the infinitesimal, splintery micro-cognitions back up my legs and my spine to my head, to make them coalesce:

W-a-O-a-W. The thought passes through me, incredibly slowly.

My body glides back down the needle at mind-blasting speed, then rockets up again, faster, towards the heavens.

I want to think, again, *Wow*, but my head is so full of the sky and the massive, impassive gold desert, it won't let words in.

I can see the whole world.

And it is beautiful.

All of it.

Before we leave for the airport to fly back to England, Mark and I head over to the Liberace Lounge in the Tropicana Hotel. There, if we pay thirteen dollars each – and can rise above the roar of the glitzed-up, automated piano, its keys plinking up and down under a waltz of frenetic, invisible fingers – we can eat as many Alaskan king crab legs as we like.

Just next to the restaurant is the escalator, eternally buzzing and mind-bendingly framed in wall-to-wall, floor-to-roof mirrors. Down it floats yet another of Vegas's white-fluffed brides – an infinity of brides, if you count her image, bouncing back and forth, in the mirrors all around. While Mark crowds the table with countless Alaskan king crab legs, I gaze at the bride, deposited, alone, at the bottom of the escalator. She has ginger candyfloss hair and unhappy skin and a bouquet of purple plastic flowers, held out in front of her, like a divining instrument.

'Oh, boy.' I watch as she begins to sail, alone, back up the endlessly moving stairs. 'I hope she finds him.'

'Let's hope he's what she's looking for,' Mark says, glancing up the escalator, before digging into the crabs. 'Unbelievable!' He holds up a crab leg of Schwarzenneggerian proportions. 'Check it out!'

After shaking his head, admiring it, he cracks the exoskeleton and eats the legful of meat. Then he eats another, and another. He ingests the flesh of a dozen legs, schloop, schloop, schloop. It's like watching a film on fast-forward. There go a dozen more. They remind him of his childhood, his happy childhood in Baltimore, Maryland, where the crabs are even more glorious than these. He goes through the third dozen more slowly. Around leg number forty, the light in his eyes dims.

'I've had enough crab,' he says. Not to me, but to himself. To his stomach.

I sit opposite him, clumsily cracking into my crab legs, slowly schlooping up the succulent, arduously burgled flesh. I giggle at the sight of Mark's discarded crab shells: they fill two big buckets on the table. Dozens of ravaged, leggy pincers sticking out, like flowers. Intergalactic lilies.

I adore him.

'Isn't it surreal?' I crack open another leg, to get at the fragrant flesh. 'Eating crabs in the middle of the desert?'

Through the window I can see weirdly lush gardens, flamingoes pinking haughtily about, taking ever-so-precious steps, as if they're wearing daringly high heels. Out there, itchy-souled boys are busy tormenting penguins. Real, slow-breathing penguins who swoon through their helplessly dinner-jacketed days, chubby refugees from *The Great Gatsby*, in an icy bowl in the middle of the desert.

I blink. 'Feels like we're in a dream.'

Mark picks up a chocolate-dipped strawberry and takes a bite. 'How d'you know we're not?'

I laugh. I love it when he takes a rare step out of his capsule of rationality.

'Ouch.' Laughter makes my abdomen ache; I think I pulled something, up in the heavens.

I rest my chin in my hands and sigh. Then sigh again. All afternoon I've been sighing, amazed – at where I've been, what I've seen. That I've come back down to earth and am here, still in one piece.

'At least you've got some colour in your cheeks now.' Mark leans back, observing me. Admiring, maybe. I think he can't quite believe I did it.

'I kissed the sky!' I'd raved, trembly legged, wild-eyed, once I'd come back down.

He'd searched my face. Half frowned. 'You've turned green.'

I hadn't told him how terrified I'd felt, up there. That I'd felt I might, really might, die.

'It's a shame,' I admit now, 'I'll never be able to do the Big Shot again – knowing how it feels.'

'I thought you said it felt fantastic?'

'It did.' I nod dreamily. 'Amazing.' The fear has made my heart bigger. What I've seen has made me feel special. Beautiful.

'I'm glad I did it. But . . .' I venture a smile, but my face is not quite my own. 'It flew off,' I tell Mark, 'while I was in the sky.'

My face flew off, like a leaf from a tree.

'But my heart . . .' It's on brilliant, blue-gold fire.

A Crisis of the Flesh
Rachel Cusk

Lately I've started seeing people's doubles. There's a man doing building work on the house next door, for example, who looks exactly like Buzz Lightyear. He came round to help us with something and I saw that his eyes were as though cut out of blue cardboard. A woman I pass on the pavement every day bears an extraordinary resemblance to Christopher Reeve in *Superman*. The classroom assistant at my daughter's nursery school – it took me a few days to work it out, but I was particularly proud of this one – is the very replica of the actor Gene Wilder. She has the same faded brown frizzy hair, the same moon-face and worried brow, the same mouth that is like a clown's mouth, miming sorrow and joy.

For three years we lived in the countryside where there were no mirrors, but recently we moved back to the city and I found suddenly that I was there, in shop windows and tinted car doors, in little squares and rectangles of glass and sometimes, like a shock, in whole shimmering reflective walls that showed me to myself, though clothed, as naked. I saw myself everywhere, like a persistent ghost or some dreaded, unavoidable acquaintance: a woman who, though vaguely familiar, seemed completely unrelated to my own scrutiny and who, at least since I last saw her, had apparently undergone an unfortunate process of ruination, some spillage or breakage or terrible neglect. She had been left out in the rain of time. This person reminded me of someone. She had a double – I just couldn't think who it was. When I was nineteen a man told me I reminded him slightly of Jean Sebourg, but I didn't think it was her. Someone showed me a recent photograph of myself in which I resembled the Chancellor of the Exchequer, Gordon Brown.

But it did not escape my attention that the woman in the mirrors, though I gave her a degree of notice, seemed to be of no interest whatever to anyone else. In the countryside this had not been made clear to me: I rarely encountered other people and when I did it was usually with sensations of mutual suspicion and relief, like Crusoe and Man Friday, at the evidence of human habitation. In the countryside, a person was something you took time over. But here, on these crowded pavements, I realized that I had, without knowing it, become invisible. I don't know exactly when this happened: I think it was somewhere between the ages of thirty-three and thirty-five. It wasn't that people had particularly noticed me before, just that it was clear they apprehended my body moving through time and space as being quintessentially human. Now, young men hove up the pavement directly towards me, their eyes fixed on some distant horizon, and when they are about a foot away they step automatically to one side, having identified, it seems, an inorganic object in their path. They avoid me as they would avoid a lamp-post. When I have my children with me then the same thing happens, on a larger scale: we are an obstacle, road-works perhaps, a big hole in the pavement with traffic cones and incident tape all round and two men with hard hats on inside.

I want to talk to 'Superman', though I don't know her. She's a bit older than me, maybe forty. She wears the clothes of a Bloomsbury poet or a country lady, man-nish clothes in brown and forest green, boots and waistcoats and sometimes a knitted shawl thrown around her neck. She is tall and straight and strong. Like her double, she has a twinkle in her eye. I feel certain that she has a secret life: it may even involve anonymous acts of valour. She has an air about her that suggests she no longer concerns herself, if she ever did, with questions of self-worth.

I can't help but wonder, though, what it's like to be her, setting sail for middle age as the caped crusader. I'll bet she wasn't pretty as a girl, or even as a young woman. She didn't mind, though. With the wisdom of her immortality she knew it was a waste of time, the interrogations of the mirror, the anxious plucking and preening and arranging, the holding in and the sticking out. She knew that none of it would last. I notice, when I pass her on the street one day, that she is always smiling. Her eyes twinkle and her black hair glints in the autumn sun. I slink by her, carrying my face like the pieces of a broken plate. And because I'm invisible, I don't think she sees me.

I'm on my way to a meeting at my daughter's school. It's the middle of the day, just before lunch, and when I get there suddenly I'm not invisible any more. On the contrary: in the infants' playground, where the four- and five-year-olds spend their breaks, I am the object of a frenzy of desire. Most of them haven't seen a parent since breakfast and they are desperate. 'She's a mummy!' yells one little boy, pointing at me over the heads of the others, like a revolutionary ordering a charge. There is a minor stampede. What am I doing there, they want to know. How did I break in? They show me their new tricks, such as hanging upside down from the climbing frame. What's your name? I ask one of them. They all answer like a shot. He's called Matt! He's called Matt! He's called Matt! He's called . . . A little girl does a special twirling thing in front of me with a skipping rope. Most of them started school for the first time two weeks before and the long days make them hungry for love. For them I am full of sweetness – they can smell it, the compassion in my mother's body, my warm lap and arms. That's good, I say to the twirling girl. She stops and looks me over from top to toe. A smile, of remembering, flees across her face.

My daughters are three and four. The younger one has a dream of girlishness. Let's play princesses, she says to her sister, leading her by the hand up to their bedroom. Princesses sit and smooth their dresses over their knees, and occasionally project one pointy foot out in front of them, in order to admire the ballet shoe in which it is encased. They speak in high-pitched voices and have an air of condescension, as though to those less fortunate than themselves. You can't be a princess for that long, usually about fifteen minutes, after which bawdy laughter and loud thumping sounds can be heard from upstairs; but, like glitter, the Princess concept comes off on everything and sticks, little repeating pieces of itself that turn what is around them lacklustre and dowdy.

She is invited to a fancy dress birthday party. There are eight or so guests, all girls. Every single one is dressed as a fairy. It is a spectacle almost unsettling in its homogeneity. They pad about pinkly in their wings and tulle skirts, holding wands, while the adults – all women – try to find somewhere to put their ungainly, ill-clad bodies. Some introductions are made, during which it becomes clear that half these women are in fact the children's nannies. We are not looking good, we women. Well, the nannies look all right, they're young and they dye their hair blonde and squeeze their large healthy bodies into tight jeans; but the rest of us are falling behind, we look like people who have wandered off the path and are going round in aimless circles in the woods, becoming increasingly lost and dishevelled. Occasionally a fairy flutters over to be rearranged. I have practised a deception on my daughter – I neglected to tell her that the fancy dress concept could incorporate fairies. Instead, I procured for her a dinosaur outfit, with a thick tail covered in padded spikes and a special soft helmet thing that fastens under the chin. She looks good, but I can tell she is starting to feel uncomfortable. Already she has removed the helmet. She tries to sit on my lap but her tail gets in the way. At home she was pleased with her costume, but now her suspicions have been aroused. When she arrived everyone made a fuss of her: she is beginning to question what their notice meant. While she certainly looks different, they all choose to look the same.

I'll be honest, I don't really go for that fairy stuff: I'd much rather be the mother of a dinosaur, though I couldn't say exactly why. I suspect I feel that to be the mother of a fairy I would have to surrender my own claims to femininity. This is an ignominious admission, yet at this gathering it seems true enough. Next to their fairies, the mothers look effaced and sexless, like plain-clothed nuns. I re-script the party in my mind, dressing all the children as dinosaurs, and I see the women, who had receded like careworn anonymous shadows beyond the circle of pink, stepping forward to reclaim their fragile, lost beauty, becoming visible once more. The truth is that I have always regarded them as yellow-haired torturers, those Barbies and Cinderellas, those fairy dolls and princesses because, in spite of their fake tans and plastic hair, their unfeasible figures and docility of character, they represent a truth that smites the heart.

A Crisis of the Flesh

As a child my hair was dark and short, and my eyes were brown, not blue. All right, sonny? said the man at the supermarket, at the sweetshop. I felt ugly and yet at the same time responsible for my physical being, as though it were some constant emanation from my soul. It seemed to me that I had done something bad; and indeed later, in the all-girl purgatory of my school dormitory, it still did not occur to me that this princess business was hierarchical, that it was more material than moral, for it was plain to see that the daughters of the rich, the barristers and bankers, were the princesses and the rest of us were not.

At school we were given fodder to eat, chocolate-spread sandwiches, hunks of sponge and custard. Beneath our blue serge uniforms, in the Cambridgeshire drizzle, we erupted into puberty. We unspooled reams of genetic programming. Differentiation occurred. Some of us developed a tendency towards adornment, others towards concealment. The princesses were in the former category. They were no longer virtuous; they grew unkind. They painted their nails and applied lipgloss, and from their blonde citadel taunted those who passed for the misfortunes of their flesh. Princesses, it became clear, did not transmogrify. They stayed the same all the way through,

merely becoming improved, taller versions of themselves, like clones.

I was not like that. I was full of shame. I covered
everything; my legs and arms and neck, even my
hands. If someone had given me a hood, I'd have
worn it. I thought that if a man ever saw me as I was,
he would run away. For a long time, getting older, for
me, remained a process of acclimatization. I felt
I would never get used to the unexpected pre-
eminence of female beauty, of the superficial, the
physical; and then gradually I did, I forgot all about it
and made my peace with who I was. But when I
looked back on my teens, I used to feel only relief that
I had outgrown them. I used to think, *If that was youth,
you can keep it.*

How should I look? I ask my husband.

I don't know, he says. Maybe you should look like
Susan Sontag. You should wear a big coat.

Susan Sontag: American feminist critic, author of
Against Interpretation. There is a photograph of her
taken by Henri Cartier-Bresson in 1975. In it she is
sitting on a sofa by a window in a bare New York apartment, smoking a cigarette. The ashtray is balanced on
the sofa beside her. She's a bit like the dark-haired one

in *Cagney & Lacey*, only better-looking. She's wearing a big coat. Her arms aren't in the sleeves – she wears it draped over her shoulders like a cape while she smokes and looks out of the window at the city.

How should I look? I ask the woman in the clothes shop. Gold jewellery runs down her in rivulets. She has abundant curling blonde hair and is wearing an asymmetrical black top that covers one shoulder while leaving the other exposed. Occasionally, she moves a hand up to fiddle with her missing shoulder as though, like an amputee, under the illusion that it is still there. She regards me, appalled. How do you *want* to look? she says.

Pull your hair back from your face, says a woman friend. She scrutinizes me, expecting a miracle. It was better down, she says after a while.

Back in the clothes shop, the assistant has shut me in a changing cubicle with numerous garments. Some are striped, some are furry. One has a ruffle running down its centre, like the mane of some mythical beast.

There is a military coat with gold buttons, like a lion tamer's uniform. There is a skirt like a petticoat, diaphanous and frilled.

I am in this shop because I have a party to go to. It is a very particular party. I know it will be full of princesses, yet I do not, as I should, admit defeat. Instead, I am out pursuing what I know I will never, at thirty-six, find: a part of myself that is new; that has yet to become, to see the light, to live.

I begin to try things on. The dress with the ruffle down the middle is dramatic. For a moment I look like someone else, a participant in the Latin American heats of *Come Dancing*. Then I look like the participant's mother. When I turn sideways I look like an Italian murderess.

The military coat is okay; there is something of Terence Stamp in *Far From the Madding Crowd*. I catch sight of my face in the mirror. It is anomalous. It is white and worried and seamed with lines. Close up, in the harsh light, it is as plain as a potato. My face used to hide the way I felt: now it's always mouthing off, it's like a second head on my body, giving away all my secrets. Do the clothes make it better or worse? I think they make it worse. In the petticoat-skirt I look like a stockbroker in drag. In a series of three different dresses I look like the various household objects that

A Crisis of the Flesh

come to life in *Beauty and the Beast*. I want to ask the shop assistant what it's all about, though I don't think she knows. Presently, I break from the fastnesses of the changing rooms and find something myself. It's a brown trouser suit, and although the words *brown trouser suit* sound like the punchline of a joke of which I may be the butt, I put it on. It looks fine. That looks fine, says the assistant. I turn sideways and catch a hint of Robert Downey Jr in the Charlie Chaplin biopic. I turn again to the front. What shoes were you thinking of putting with it? the shop assistant enquires. I ask her whether I could wear my trainers and she nearly explodes. *Trainers?* she yells. She appears genuinely angry. She asks me my size and stomps off to see what she can find. Minutes later she returns with a pair of black patent-leather slingbacks with stiletto heels and toes as long and sharp as ravens' beaks. I do not have the feet of a princess. In my size, the shoes look like gondolas. They are positively frightening. I try them on, but even in this giant incarnation my feet won't fit. I shove them halfway in for form's sake and try to stand up. Susan Sontag, I am sure, would not have suffered such indignities. The shop assistant points out that most of my foot is hanging over the back of the shoe. She seems uncomfortable, as though my feet have betrayed to her the fact that I am not human but animal. She acts as though she thinks she should inform somebody. The question of my footwear is left unresolved, though I buy the suit in an attempt to pacify her. At the till she is already distracted by the next customer. For a moment, I believe I could run away – I could leave the brown heap of cloth on the counter and run through the glass doors. It would be, I feel sure, as though I were shrugging off the cast of time itself. Thank you, I say to her as she hands me the bag. At the sound of my voice she turns her face to me and her vapid pale blue eyes half-register something, I don't know what. It is as though I have pricked her, or disturbed her sleep. Enjoy it, she says.

Having any more? people say at the school gate, in the playground. They're talking about children.

No, I say emphatically. I say it emphatically not out of strong feeling but because there are already too many questions to which I don't know the answer.

Oh, they say wistfully. Well, you're probably very sensible.

How about you? I say. Having any more?

Ha, well, I don't know, no, I mean, well probably not. Sometimes I think I'd quite like to, you know, squeeze in one more. But no, probably not.

A Crisis of the Flesh

Oh well, I say.

At the playground the leaves have turned brown and yellow. They lie around the trees in rings on the grass, like little piles of shorn golden hair. Sometimes the wind lifts them up and whirls them around. The children sit on the swings and go back and forth.

I just can't bear the idea of saying, you know, *this is it*, says one woman to another.

I know, the other one says. I know. It's like, and now I'm just going to get older and older and then . . .

I can't quite follow what they're saying. I am often bewildered by the ability some mothers have in conversation, to move from head lice to mortality in a matter of seconds.

When are we middle-aged? I ask.

Menopause, they both reply, smart as whips.

When are we middle-aged? I ask a younger friend, a woman.

When you can't just go out and get a man like *that*, she says. She snaps her fingers imperatively in the air.

How old do you think I am? I ask my daughters.

There is a long silence.

Are you twelve? ventures one.

*

When my daughters were born I felt each time as though my whole life had gathered itself up, had made a leap such as a dancer might make or like a soprano hitting her highest note. I had an exultant sense of reaching the centre; of standing on the pinnacle around which the years arranged themselves in steeps and slopes and foothills. These were moments of truth, though they are growing a little distant now, three years, four – they stand in my life like a vista of mountains, immobile, full of remote, intricate grandeur. I could return there, but I don't want to. Sometimes I thirst to live one of those exultant hours again, but I don't have it in me. I know how each voyage to that strange sierra wears you out. You come back depleted.

In hospital, for a few hours afterwards, I remember a distinct sensation of unearthliness, almost of immortality. Yet the feeling passed: such mysteries as those of which I was at that time the vessel are by their nature transient. They pass through the raw furrow of remembered pain, grandly, royally, like a princess along a red regal carpet, and they do not return. And it was perhaps in the wake of that gracious lady, that giver of life, that I began to look in the mirror at myself and see – what? The past?

Walking along the road a car draws to a halt beside

me. It is a big family car. It is sort of hunched and armoured: it is a protective shell, like that of an armadillo. The door opens and a girl steps out onto the pavement in front of me. She is young, no more than twelve or thirteen. She has recently cast off her childhood: she has emerged from its abstractions with guns blazing. She is all tossing hair and clicking heels, all sullenness and tiny handbag. Inside the car sits her mother. I see her briefly through the open door and she sees me. She is leaning over the gear stick to say something to her daughter. The mother is wearing the assemblage of anomalous garments that go under the heading 'tracksuit'. Her hair is short and her face is careworn. She is overweight, unmade-up, ungroomed. She is a monument to discarded love. She mouths some imprecation to her daughter and her daughter ignores her. I suddenly see the girl as a looter, leaving the car with her arms full of stolen things. The mother meets my gaze with an intensity that is almost alarming. Then the girl slams the door on her and tick-tacks off up the street.

In France they do things differently, don't they? Once, years ago, I saw a Frenchwoman slap her daughter's cheeks. I confronted her, Neanderthal but well intentioned, like the Yeti in *Star Wars*. *Non*, I said, shaking my head at the mother, while the little girl stared at me, terrified. *Non, non*. The woman was thin and coiffed and as neat as a new pin. Vaguely I took in her co-ordinated handbag and shoes, her mascara'ed stare. She didn't seem to know what on earth I was talking about. Presently, she shrugged and walked off, shooing the little girl in front of her.

The pharmacies in France are full of creams and potions. As far as I can see, in that country *jeunesse* is understood to be an entirely superficial phenomenon. It is a mere matter of discipline and money, neither of which are particularly youthful characteristics – *au contraire*, in France maturity may well be the key ingredient of *jeunesse*. In the town, at the beach, along the coastal path, everywhere people are playing tennis, jogging, exercising. One woman sits on her beach towel doing an elaborate form of kinesthetics, or is it yoga? She balances on her pelvis and raises her arms and legs vertically in a compressing motion, like a human paperclip. This year, in the water, French women do not swim, but rather stride up and down in the shallows with the lumbering gait of Arctic explorers. This activity seems full of scientific import, the motive for which can only, I think, be that of *jeunesse*. As far as I know there is no other recognized cause in France for abandoning one's vanity. In the cafe at the top of the beach, a group of pregnant women sit smoking cigarettes around a table. Unlike all the other women here, they are laughing loudly. The smoking and the laughing seem deliberate, of a piece: they are a form of camouflage for the riotousness of reproduction itself. They express, in a way, embarrassment. The women are styling themselves – on their table, it's all about excess. I don't doubt that once they've got rid of their cargo they'll be back earnestly fording the shallows with the others.

As a child I stayed with a French family in Paris on an exchange programme. There was *maman*, *papa*, a daughter my age and a younger boy. *Maman* did not wear tracksuits. She was very handsome. Her lean, muscled form moved about the house with the stealth of a high-fashion panther. She smoked constantly and had a low voice and a diffident, understated manner. She and *papa* were often to be found in a passionate clinch, in the kitchen, in the hall. Their bathroom bristled with house plants and with her pharmaceutical exotica. They kept a silver ashtray where the soap dish should have been. She was cultured and intelligent and good-humoured and she produced minuscule, beautiful meals over which we conversed *en famille*.

She was the same age that I am now. I admired her very much, yet her supremacy was in numerous ways frightening to me. I had never before met a woman – a mother – like her. There was about her no warm, tyrannical miasma of partiality. To be with her involved no unpersoning, no trespass into intimate spheres of jurisdiction. There was no fleshly indignity. There was no atmosphere of sacrifice. I couldn't believe she *was* a mother. She was more like a sort of older friend. It was, I suppose, the combination of her self-containment and her glamour; the fact that she drew notice without offering an emotional harbour. In her house I felt inchoate, formless, needy. I wept with homesickness yet at the same time desired to be where I was, to be cured of my emotion and encircled by the rightness of her taste; to be made by association beautiful. Yet I see now that her world was separated from mine by straits of impossible narrowness. In her world, sentiment was its own punishment. In mine, beauty was its own reward.

And her daughter, my friend? She was a pious girl of great propriety. Her ambition at the time was to be a nun. I don't doubt, looking back, that she disapproved of her mother.

*

A Crisis of the Flesh

We sit next to a woman and her daughter on the train. It is a long journey, from Edinburgh down south, and the train is small and crowded and running very late; and we haven't brought enough food and in a quiet voice the woman says to me, Look, would they like some of these? She holds out two little packets of Jaffa Cakes, special small novelty ones the size of ten-pence pieces. Her nails are curved like scimitars, painted with red lacquer. They are like a family of exotic insects. She is suntanned and she has very long, very straight shiny hair. I noticed her earlier: she is not invisible. I saw her bring out a bag of fresh peas, which she podded and put delicately in her mouth.

Oh, I say, that's very kind, are you sure your little girl won't want them? We speak in whispers, two smugglers trading contraband. Don't worry, says the woman. Look. She holds back her long hair and bends over to pull out a large plastic box from under the seat. It looks like something you might carry on a lifeboat rescue. I bend over too to look while she lifts the lid. Inside are dozens of the little Jaffa packets packed together in orange rows like ingots, and other things too – at least twenty sandwiches cut into little squares, serried ranks of carrot sticks, cloud banks of crisp packets, infinite subdivisions of things wrapped in foil, in cellophane. It is a whole world, a packed lunch planet. Oh my God, I say. I know, she says. And it's all for *her* – she indicates the little girl, who is staring silently out of the window at the Borders, the sunlight flashing on her face. Who did it? I say. The woman looks at me. *My mother*, she whispers.

I write to a distant friend, asking for her thoughts on middle age. She writes back. Why would I have such thoughts? she says. Middle age is a long way away.

Don't call it middle age, then. Call it a crisis of the flesh.

It is said that men assuage their feelings of mortality by seeking out relationships with younger women. And women? What do they do?

At the department store, the escalators are made of perspex or glass, so that you can see their human freight as it is circulated through the many-layered centre of the building. It is like an illustration of the chambers of the heart, with customers streaming in and then emerging, oxygenated by shopping. The department store is in a shopping centre that sits in a vast web of roads, adjacent to a motorway. The cafe on the top floor is full of people. There are a few elderly couples, but most of the people are women. I once heard a man say that it was impossible for a middle-aged woman to be attractive. As though this epithet had inspired some fascistic form of social legislation, the middle-aged women are up here, in hiding. The man didn't mean you couldn't be fond of a middle-aged woman – just that you wouldn't choose one, out of all the world's maidens. In the cafe the women are mainly in twos, lunching. Beside them lie numerous large glossy carrier bags, like recumbent hounds at the feet of princesses. Most of them appear to be discussing the state of play. They refer neither to the past – that's for the elderly couples, happy as babies in their chairs – nor to the future, but offer descriptions of an unending present, like commentators on a horse race. They talk about their husbands as though they were their children and their children as though they were their husbands. They talk about their houses and their holidays. They are well turned out, as if against the possibility of a random event touching their lives.

I am not here for solace, nor for lunch: I am here to purchase a school uniform for my stepdaughter. We ride up and down the escalators, searching for the appropriate department. An atmosphere bordering on mayhem pervades the building. The excitement is most concentrated around the floor devoted to women's clothing, where, as we pass, I see that a fashion show is in progress. A model picks her way up and down a platform, as exotic as an animal from the zoo. Dark hair cascades down her lissom back and when she shows us her painted face it is as though she were showing us a picture, a landscape in oils. At her feet sits an audience of middle-aged women. They gaze at her as she struts up and down. Every so often she returns to the back of the platform to look at herself in a long mirror. She shakes her mane of hair and pivots herself about. It is evident that she enjoys looking at herself, and who can blame her? The envious compere, a tired-looking woman with dirty blonde highlights, gives a commentary on the model's various outfits. From the escalator, the scene reminds me of the fairies' party, except worse. There is something predatory about the silent, speculating audience, the compere's assessing monologue. They think, for a moment, that they own this girl and her strangely synthetic beauty.

We are levitated up to shoes, where children are running riot and a woman in a purple suede coat is periscoping her permed head around and shouting, *Claudia! Claudia!* and a huge queue simmering with unrest snakes all the way round to lingerie. Shoes, I suppose, can wait. We descend to the basement. There I find the relevant rack of uniforms, but we are late and their stocks are depleted. There is a uniform for

A Crisis of the Flesh

a moose, and a uniform for a mouse, but nothing in between. A large, Brunhilda-like woman with her hair in a Tyrolean plait has drawn near and begins to scour my rack with her white tapered fingers. Her daughter stands beside her, quiet and correct. I tell them there is nothing there, but the woman elbows me aside and flays the rack all the same. It is the last day of the holidays. I open my mouth to say that I'm glad someone else is as dilatory as me, but the woman speaks first. We just popped in, she says, to think about perhaps getting one or two extra jerseys. Oh, I say to the girl, so you've got your uniform already? She nods. Outside it is a beautiful day. I wonder why they are here in this purgatory when they could be free, heading west with the top down and their Tyrolean plaits coming loose in the wind. Well, I say to my stepdaughter, at least we can get some tights, they're bound to have those. You'll have to start school tomorrow in something else. It's not tomorrow, chorus the mother and daughter. It's the day after.

I can't find the tights, and I can't find anyone to tell me where they are. I join the queue, which is long and consists of many identical units, each made up of a middle-aged woman and an eleven-year-old girl. They stand side by side in two replicating lines, like an exhibition of Russian dolls. I listen to their conversation. The uniform department is hot and windowless. There is nothing in it to please the eye or lift the spirit. With its looted racks it resembles the scene of some recent anarchy. It resembles my soul. When I reach the front of the queue, I ask the man at the till where I can find tights. Because I am invisible, he barely raises his head. Try shoes, he says. Third floor.

Have you been to shoes? I ask him.

He looks up. No, he says.

I have, I say. And if I have to go back there I am going to throw myself off the roof.

As one, the women in the queue behind me stand to attention. Down there! they yell, bristling their arms out to make signposts. Third aisle, on the left! Their tone is urgent. Threats of suicide are clearly common down here, and are taken seriously.

Thank you, I say.

Is there anything else, madam? says the man behind the till.

Yes, I say. I need a school uniform.

Right you are, says the man. I'll just get the floor manager.

He summons Camilla Parker-Bowles, and immediately dispatches her to find what I require in the stockroom. She returns a matter of minutes later with all the right things. All this while, the women have been standing in the queue behind me, waiting hopefully, as if wanting to see the story end well. With their small round eyes and inquisitive noses they remind me of a herd of geese.

Outside it is a beautiful day, the last but one of summer.

And then we go to a dinner party. We walk, as it isn't far. In any case, we rarely drive when we go out in the evening. I refuse, not because I am averse to sobriety but because going out in a car makes me feel old. It makes me feel like my parents. It makes me feel immured. I like to return from an evening at least a little dishevelled – cycling is perfect, but walking will do.

The other guests are a balding IT consultant and his wife, a solicitor. He is toothy and shiny and red, with a head like a well-risen loaf. In fact, he bears a certain resemblance to Dr Romano in *ER*. She is like a paper pattern held together with pins at the seams: she rustles, and seems as though she might tear. They are old. They are at least a hundred. The talk is of schools and help, schools and help. At some point in the evening I discover that they are not a hundred. They are thirty-eight and thirty-nine. On the subject of help, our hostess mentions a Taiwanese girl who once lived with their family. She filled the house with her friends, who cooked Taiwanese dishes in the kitchen. It was lovely, the exotic smells, the youthful, unintelligible chatter. Dr Romano guffaws. Darling, he says to the Paper Doll, what about Jane and Geoff? Shall we tell them about Jane and Geoff? Jane and Geoff, he continues, addressing the group, have an eighteen-year-old Italian au pair who looks *just like Sophia Loren*. He folds his arms and sits back in his chair, beaming redly. The Paper Doll rustles and gives a parchment smile. The talk immediately returns to schools. Presently Dr Romano tries again. This time he addresses his remarks to his host. I was round there the other day, he says, and my friend Geoff answered the door. So Geoff looks at me and he says – Dr Romano puts on Geoff's voice, which is gruff, and his expression, which is urgent – he says, *I think you'd better come in for coffee.* You'd better come in for coffee! Huh huh! Dr Romano guffaws loudly. The Paper Doll is pretending not to listen.

Well, I say to Dr Romano, it's no wonder women feel worthless and unattractive as they get older. It's no big surprise, is it?

Dr Romano has not addressed a word to me all evening, and he doesn't start now.

Oh, you women, sighs our host. He rolls his eyes.

A Crisis of the Flesh

You all worry too much. You don't know your own beauty. You don't know your power.

I ask Dr Romano whether he feels middle-aged. Not really, he snaps, no.

The host and I talk for a while. The conversation has journeyed a little way when Dr Romano begins to speak.

I work with a lot of younger guys, he says, and there's no real difference between them and me. Not really. Anyway, I try not to let them see that there is. It's hard – I mean, most of them don't even have *children*. Well, one or two of them do but they're little babies, you know, not actual children, and when they find out that I've got *three* and that one of them's actually at *secondary* school, well, it's pretty much impossible to hide the fact that I'm, you know, *older* than them, even though I go to the gym. Sometimes, if I collect the children from school I think, huh, I hope no one from work sees me! They wouldn't believe it! Actually, they just have to look at the photos on the desk, he says bleakly. Then they add it up.

When you're sixty, someone tells me, you'll feel silly for having wasted thirty-six feeling old. I don't want to feel silly.

There is poverty and there is suffering. There is injustice, pain, ugliness, hatred. And there are youth and beauty, but I never thought they were important. I thought they were trivial. I thought they were over-rated.

There's a look I'm after – 'Superman' gave me the idea. It's sort of androgynous, sort of New Romantic. It was how I wanted to look when I was a teenager, before thoughts of womanhood ensnared me and led me into that scented labyrinth of mirrored cubicles. Sort of Lou Reed meets the Three Musketeers, in a Parisian cafe frequented by French intellectuals.

Something like that.

The First Boy I Loved
Sophie Dahl

Saturday night at the Dome in Tufnell Park, the Pixies singing 'Gigantic'; Gemma, Mirry and I wearing Doc Marten boots, short, tasselled miniskirts and skinny-rib tops from Camden Market.

They both had long dark hair, clouds of it. I had a short blonde bob, and when boys were chatting me up they told me I looked like Patsy Kensit from Eighth Wonder.

Gemma and Mirry smoked B&H, and I occasionally smoked Honeyrose cigarettes, which you could buy in the chemist, tasted like bonfires and gave you a sore throat.

We all drank snakebite and black, and the boys took cheap speed, which made their mouths dry and eyes wide and they didn't dance, just sat leaning against the walls, tapping their feet relentlessly and tracing patterns against our arms with clammy fingers.

Every Friday night I would stand shivering in the

line, fake ID in hand, anxious to be in the moist darkness, so hot even the floors were sweating. Every Saturday morning I would make the pilgrimage to Camden Market from Battersea on the Northern Line, to buy bootleg Nirvana tapes and Levi's that were violet or bruise-blue.

It was a blowsy September morning when I went to meet Mirry for this weekly ritual, shortly after my fifteenth birthday. She was standing outside Camden Tube with some boys I knew and one I didn't. He had the greenest eyes I'd ever seen and a nose like a centurion. An air of mystery clung to him, and he seemed coolly detached from his friends, surveying them all with wry amusement. His eyes fixed on me.

'All right?' he said.

I blushed and looked at the sky a lot. When they left, I fired a stream of questions at Mirry. Who was he, where did he go to school, did he have a girlfriend?

He was at Westminster. No Girlfriend.

His name was Jack. And everyone fancied him.

The following Saturday, after a week of replaying the meeting in my head again and again, a plan had been orchestrated. I told my mother I was staying the night with my friend Eve. Mikhel had a house without any parents in it and we were going to meet Jack at Sloane Square tube at ten o'clock.

I felt like a Russian romantic, except I was wearing hot-pants, a silk shirt stolen from my stepfather, a pair of laddered tights and platforms from Shelley's Shoes. We click-clacked down the Kings Road: Eve, who looked like a Rossetti painting; Mikhel, who I'd known since I was little and liked to be called Mike so people didn't think he was posh; and me, terrified but overwhelmed by anticipation and a lusty dose of teenage passion.

A lone figure stood on the platform. My heart lurched as he sauntered over, cocked his head towards me, and smiled. 'Sophie,' he said.

'Hello,' I muttered.

We walked down the road, the four of us, sharing a bottle of cheap vodka. As we neared Battersea Bridge, he reached for my cold hand with his, stroking my fingers.

Eve and Mikhel took acid when we arrived at his house, and while they went to count how many stairs there were, Jack assembled a spliff with military precision, then told me to sit on his lap, where he kissed me very thoroughly.

'Let's go upstairs,' he said, after a while, hot-eyed.

Mikhel's bedroom was small, with rave posters on the wall and elephant-smattered curtains from the General Trading Company. He still had bunk beds.

The First Boy I Loved

My boy of few words pulled me into the bottom bunk where we slept half clothed, legs entangled.

Mikhel's mother woke us up in the morning, apoplectic with rage, unexpectedly home. Jack shielded my left breast, which had caught her attention. 'I know about you,' she said to me, ominously. 'I'm going to telephone your mother.'

I was half laughing and half crying as Jack walked me home. 'Oh God, oh shit, she *will* call my mother—'

'Sophie,' he interrupted, 'will you go out with me?'

I tried not to smile. 'Yes,' I said.

When I walked through the front door, my mother was in the kitchen, making coffee, smoking a cigarette, giggling on the phone. She waved. The kitchen smelled like croissants and fun.

'Hi, baby,' she said.

I came clean, terrified. She threw back her lovely bewitching head and roared with laughter; unpredictable, as always.

'Silly old cow,' she said, when I told her about Mikhel's mother. 'So is Jack your boyfriend?'

'Yeah, he is.' I grinned, went upstairs and wrote I LOVE JACK over everything I owned.

*

After a while, my mother became suspicious. At thirty-four, her father had died the year before and she was engulfed by swamps of black depression, coupled with episodes of rage and fury that left us all edgy, never sure of how she'd wake up.

I spent hours on the phone crooning to Jack, and when he came over I would lock my bedroom door and he would take off my clothes, stroking my body with such wonder and care that I felt swollen and drunk, deep as a well.

My mother didn't like it: Jim Morrison blasting from my room; locked doors and love bites; the high giddy hormones pulsing through her house. She didn't recognize me as her shy English good daughter. I was a wanton.

She was taking pills and her handbag rattled and she could get as angry as a snake. 'I don't want that boy in my house,' she hissed, furious, one day.

'But why?'

'Because it's very clear to me that you're having sex.'

'I'm not!' I shouted. And I wasn't – I clung to my virginity tenaciously, like a Mills and Boon heroine.

'Don't lie to me, you slut,' and she slapped me hard across the face. I felt removed, as though I was watching a soap opera.

'You'd better leave,' I told Jack, weeping with shame for my mother and for myself.

'I'll talk to her,' he said, thin arms protectively around me.

'She won't listen – you should just go.'

He left as she shrieked like a wraith along the hall after him, and then he loped awkwardly down Henning Street, disappearing into the winter.

It was around this time that my mother decided boarding school was a better place for me to be and we endured silent car journeys through rural England, to serene villages and schools behind gates with leafy tree-lined driveways where people thought it was cool to sit in a field with a bottle of Cinzano, hid in the bushes to smoke, and snogged each other in a freezing graveyard. It did not seem like fun to me. I picked the school that was nearest to a train station, should I need to run away.

My mother and I reached a polite yet uneasy stalemate. Boarding school would start after the Christmas holidays.

Jack reassured me and I met him every day after school, kissing in tube stations and the shopping centres round Victoria. Occasionally, I had the luxury of spending the night with him, and we would stay at the houses of unchaperoned friends in various cold-sheeted guest rooms, Peter Jones-y and chaste. I would pack a sexy nightdress, face cream and a toothbrush, and we would play at being a proper couple.

At a party in Oxford we found ourselves in another bed, but at the crucial moment I said, 'I don't know about this actually – STOP.' But I still went to the loo afterwards to see if I looked different, and my cheeks and eyes shone in the mirror.

We went downstairs to join the florid throng, and amidst teenagers throwing whipped cream and tequila at each other, Jack got furious with me and accused me of flirting with his friend Tom (I was). We walked outside into the silent night, me protesting.

'The problem is,' he said, 'I wouldn't mind, but I've fallen in love with you. I love you.'

Every star lit up like the Pirates of the Caribbean ride at Disneyland. I was filled with reeling dizzy joy and when our housekeeper came to pick me up at midnight – my curfew – I sat in the car, hot needles shooting down my body, making me twist and curl, breathing in deeply like I had a secret.

It was, sadly, the friend Tom who would be the beginning of the end of the story.

He wrote bad poetry and talked a lot.

The First Boy I Loved

I called him, who knows why, and one Sunday afternoon I made my way to his house, a long journey involving trains and buses and taxis and getting lost by a biscuit factory; long enough to think about the fact that I was about to do something wrong and irreversible, but I still did it.

Our kiss was brief and unfamiliar. The moment it happened I realized I had made a dreadful mistake. 'Please don't tell Jack,' I begged. But as is the wont of fifteen-year-old boys, he did, in the common room at school the next day.

'I got off with your girlfriend last night and she loved it,' he announced to Jack and an audience.

My silent brave boyfriend called me at lunchtime. 'It doesn't matter,' he said. 'I still love you.'

Yet it did matter, and after that the whole thing was sour and our conversations waned and when he said, 'I love you,' I muttered glumly, 'Me too.'

On Thanksgiving night he called me. He was cold. My mother was having a dinner party. 'I've had it,' he said flatly. 'You're a bitch and I hate you.'

'OK, Jack, that's fine. I understand,' I said gaily, and hung up.

I went downstairs and regaled my mum and her friends with a dramatic account, and they all roared with laughter. Under the table my legs were shaking and I felt odd. When I went to bed I cried, pressing my fist into my mouth, swallows beating in my chest.

He got his revenge two years later. The country air had not improved my looks. My game confidence was gone. I was no longer lean and sparkly-eyed. My body had betrayed me, suddenly ungainly and complicated. My virginity had been lost, in an ardent but careless moment.

I went to a party and got steaming drunk with some girlfriends from school. In the sitting room I saw Jack smoking a joint, eyes like slits, with a tiny-hipped pretty little thing dancing around him like a butterfly.

I stumbled over. 'Can I talk to you?'

'I'll meet you outside in a moment,' he said, bored. I waited and waited on a stairwell, smoking one cigarette after another, but he never came. An hour later he ran past me with his friends, laughing.

'You've got fat,' he spat out at me, as they fell about like the crows in *Dumbo*.

'Jack,' I called, thickly.

'Fuck off,' he replied. I did.

*

When I was nineteen, going everywhere, every night, red lipstick, drunk and stoned and oh, so hopeful, ordering bottles of champagne and dancing to 'white lines don't do it' on tabletops, everything was fast and frenzied and *not enough*.

I was standing in the loo at the Café de Paris on a Wednesday night. I looked in the mirror. Green eyes were on me. We glanced at each other warily, then laughed. 'Do you want to leave, Jack?' I asked, nervous of his rebuff.

'Yes,' he said.

We bought champagne and strangely half-frozen strawberries from Harts the Grocers, and ran like schoolchildren to Thurloe Square where we broke into the communal gardens. A midsummer rainstorm caught us and we fell into each other like little wolves, lightning flashing above us, illuminating everything.

A shy courtship progressed over the next few weeks and he came by train to stay at my mother's house in Oxfordshire. It was a turbulent time – three days before she tried to kill herself – a dark and wretched time. We had supper at midnight in the garden, a hot, close English summer night. My mother was disorientated and paranoid and Jack placated her softly, and was very kind to my eleven-year-old brother, who was riddled with confusion.

Later, as we lay in bed, he told me that he still loved me, that nothing had changed. I came with a litany of excuses, the real truth eluding me, that I was frightened and adrift. He looked at me with tired compassion.

'When are you going to be honest, Sophie?' he said. I asked him to go and sleep upstairs, and lay in the darkness for a long time, dry-eyed and still.

On our return to London, I said I would ring later, and I didn't. I ended up in a bar in Soho with a collection of night people, fast flighty people, who I was trying to impress. Looking up from my drink, I saw Jack, standing in front of me, someone from another time. I did not invite him to join us and we had a brief exchange, me willing him to leave, which he did, with that same fast loping walk, down Wardour Street and beyond.

That night I hated myself, and him for loving me with my fucked-up family and half truths; Jack who knew I used cold cream and was a bit of a dork really; that it was as easy as anything to make me blush; that I loved *Top of the Pops* and didn't really know how to dance to rave music.

And at sunrise, I sat in a formerly grand hotel room with a bunch of people who weren't my friends, eating cheese sandwiches and trading dawn confidences with a guitarist; me weeping wordlessly for my mother and for us all, he crying out of solidarity or God knows what. And I thought then that a chapter had been closed, to be put away in a dusty and forgotten nursery.

Yet Jack is and always will be an indelible part of my youth – a smudgy reminder of that innocence, those inexplicable lurching moments of joy and lust and confusion and heady heat that is fifteen. That when thought of now, fills me with a mournful ache for what has been, like smoky autumn mornings in London, the smell of earth after a summer storm, and pictures of my little brothers and sister in their first school uniforms. It's a feeling so vast it makes you tiny, with all the sense and wonder that feels like being born.

At Sea Sabine Durrant

This is what I know about my father.

1   He liked reading Georgette Heyer. (His name, M. J. W. Durrant, is inscribed in a hardback copy of *The Unknown Ajax*.)

2   He played squash, and didn't like it when he lost. (My mother's uncle told me that.)

3   He was a fighter pilot, a lieutenant, in the Fleet Air Arm. At one point, his aircraft carrier was the *Ark Royal*. (There used to be a photo of the *Ark Royal* in our front room.)

4   He smoked. (Photographic evidence of this.)

5   He also had a purpley-blue polo neck which someone must have knitted him. (I found this in a cupboard.)

6   His mother died when he was a baby. His

father, a piano teacher, remarried three times and had six more children. (Family fact.)

7   He was killed flying off the Dorset coast in 1964. He was twenty-nine. His body was never found. (Ditto.)

These are the people I imagined might be my father when I was small:

1   Alan Alda.
2   Hutch (the blond one, played by David Soul, in the 1970s cop series *Starsky and Hutch*).
3   My father's half-brother Jeremy, who used to visit us until he got married and moved away.
4   D'Artagnan in the 1970s cartoon version of *The Four Musketeers*.

It is 20 January 2003, a gloomy day. Cars hiss over the speedbump outside our house. It's my birthday. I am thirty-nine. I'm trying to work. My youngest son, home from nursery, keeps coming in and out of my study. He wants to know where his sunglasses are.

'Your ones that were broken,' he says. 'The ones you gave me.'

I tell him where they might be, and he wanders off. He's always filching things from me: a bit of jewellery here, a scarf, a notebook, my gloves. It can be annoying – I only gave him the sunglasses after *he* broke them – but touching at the same time. I wonder what it's about. It's probably not that he likes collecting things of mine, more that these things help him to play at being grown-up. Not like the home-knit polo-neck jumper (moth-eaten now, the purpley-blue fading to mauve), smuggled a long time ago from my mother's wardrobe and now carefully folded in my drawer; or the appropriated Georgette Heyer hardback on my shelf; or the photographs, slipped out of other people's albums when they weren't looking, in the box by my bed.

I find myself thinking about my father. This isn't odd, or unusual. I find myself thinking about him all the time. What is odd is what I *find* to think about. There is an absence, a hole, a not knowing. I know little about his life, or what he was like, still less about his death. There is no body, no gravestone. His relations are dead, scattered or disassociated. His photograph went a long time ago from my mother's mantelpiece. A relative recently distributed a home-made family tree and his name wasn't there. Even before my mother's remarriage twenty-seven years ago, he wasn't a regular topic of conversation. The only person who ever really talked about him was my great-uncle on my mother's side, a lover of opera and sentiment, given to spouting poetry and deliciously embellished stories, who was drawn to him, it seemed, out of a sense of romance. But even he would only bring up his name when we were alone. I was a baby when my father died; by the time I was old enough to understand, everyone else had 'moved on'.

I thought I wasn't *supposed* to ask. Instead, I picked things up piecemeal – information, objects. I knew there was something mysterious about his 'accident', that the navy was involved. He flew planes, though, and the navy was about boats, so sometimes I'd think maybe I'd got it wrong and he was in the RAF. I thought probably he was killed in a war, though I wasn't sure what war it was in 1964, or what this war was doing in Lyme Bay.

There was a documentary about the *Ark Royal* on television in the seventies and I taped the music – Rod Stewart's 'I Am Sailing' – and listened to it, in secret, under the covers of my bed. I stole books with his name, Lt M. J. W. Durrant – the M stood for Michael, but the 'J' and the 'W'? – on the flyleaf (not just the

Regency romance but *The Navy at War* by Captain S. W. Roskill, RN, and a manual entitled *Knots, Splices and Fancy Work*); also a folder of his school essays I subsequently lost and for which, even now, visiting my mother's house, I find myself searching; and a paisley silk dressing gown, and the photographs, and the jumper, and stowed them away under my bed. At school, I made up stories. I could keep a whole table rapt at lunch with vivid descriptions of his death – my spoon plunging from a great height into a sea of chocolate sauce. It made me feel special, sort of heroic myself. Refer to only having a mother in a poem or a story and I knew I'd get a gentle smile from the teacher and a gold star. And when I was a bit older, in my teens, very little changed. I found nothing imposed instant gravitas, *depth*, on a late-night conversation with a prospective lover like the retelling of childhood tragedy. I knew that not having a father, having no grasp of what it meant to have one, made me sad, but the sadness was solid – there was something to hold on to in it. I didn't know what I was missing.

Why isn't this enough any more? I don't know what has changed recently but the sadness isn't solid any more. The loss feels real and acute. My children were watching the 'sequel' to Disney's *Peter Pan* the other day and when at the end the girl's father returns from war, I found myself sobbing. It's a cartoon, a limp one at that, and I couldn't stop. What is this? Is it that I'm thirty-nine – which, it strikes me, is exactly ten years older than my father when he died? Or that I watch my two sons grow up, every day, with a father of their own? I'm pregnant again, too, and in the wash of hormones, the sense of fresh vulnerability is a terrible morbidity. I never knew my father. My father never knew his mother. Rationally, I know there's no reason for such bad luck to continue, but my imagination can't help it. Will one of my children never know me? I'm sitting here trying to write a third novel in which it seems, yet again, the main character has an absent or dead father. Why do I think I can write about siblings, of which I have none, but fathers seem out of bounds *unimaginable*? And yet the need to imagine him is so powerful it consumes me.

Or perhaps it is something else, to do with the threat of war in Iraq, the talk of troops and aircraft carriers, the training in progress in corners of rural England. Recently, I've been forced to confront certain assumptions I carry side by side in my head. From the liberal, left-wing standpoint I like to believe I conduct my life, I know what kind of person becomes a military officer – right wing, upper class, dim. But then there is M. J. W. Durrant. In my diary for 1976, I wrote of my mother's new husband, 'He's only a businessman. Not like my father, who fought for his country.' It's a belief I hold unexamined. If anyone else told me proudly they 'fought for their country', I'd tell them to get a life, or at least a proper job. But my father is suspended in amber. I may have known nothing about him, but I have long ago made him what I wanted, merging what he *did* into what he *was*: a great man, a hero with the body, as my mother's uncle once said, of 'a Greek god'. And if this idolization came to seem reductive, there were other models to co-opt: a wise-cracking cop, a celluloid musketeer, a character in *M.A.S.H.*

But none of this, the heroism of the man, or the daughter, makes me feel special, or interesting, any more. It makes me feel empty, and tearful, and unsure of myself. I have so many questions. Where was he born? What are the facts, the dates of his life? What was the texture? When exactly did he die? Was his body, and the wreckage of his plane, really never discovered, or was it, as my great-uncle once said, a cover-up? Why has no one found out? And what was he like? Was he right-wing? Was he racist? Did he believe in capital punishment? Would I even be talking to him today?

Joe is still looking for my sunglasses. The streets are wet. It is one of those days that never gets light. What use is my box of mementoes, the dilapidated hand-knit sweater that may have meant no more to him than my broken sunglasses do to me, if I know none of this? I am thirty-nine, ten years older than my father when he died. It won't wash any more.

I'm old enough to know better.

Actually, I *think* he was twenty-nine when he died. I don't even know that for sure.

The obvious place to start is my mother. I decide not to start here. There are honourable, and less honourable, reasons for this. There is the weight of the *not* talking, for one thing, the embarrassment of bringing his name up after all this time. Does this sound odd? I don't even know how to ask. 'I wonder if you could tell me about Michael?': too formal. 'Mike', too intimate. 'My dad': unthinkable. Even, 'My father' the obvious, fraught with problems, as if I was asserting some kind of right over him.

I used to think I remembered the night he didn't come back. I know there was a knock at the door, and that the commander would have been standing there. I've seen officers in police dramas do the same. But I have a memory of the high kitchen stools we had in that house and a neighbour, and my mother sobbing, retching, in a place beyond reach. But of course it can't be that night. I was only a few months old. It must have happened when I was older. A year later perhaps, or two, one evening when grief caught her up again.

I don't want to upset her. I know it's thirty-nine years, and that for twenty-seven of them she has been married to someone else, but I don't want to make her cry.

And also – and this is something I feel uncomfortable admitting to – I need to find out about him on my own. I don't want information filtered through my mother. I want to possess him for myself.

There's a woman on her mobile phone in Births in the Family Records Centre in Farringdon. A man, another researcher, comes over and berates her. 'Can't you read the signs?' he snaps. 'Are you blind?'

Of course she isn't blind. You can't be blind in the Family Records Centre. You have to use your eyes all the time. You scan. You flick. Up and down. Across. And back. You shunt the great books in and out of the shelves. You take them out and put them back in the right place. There is a huge sound of repeated shunting, clunking, rustling, a sort of percussion.

Naively, I'd thought you just put a name into a computer and all the information you needed would spew out. But you need dates. I don't have any dates. But in Births I'm lucky. I sift through the books for 1935 – my first guess – and, in March, I find a Durrant, M. J., born in Bournemouth. There is no W in his initials, but it is close enough not to be a coincidence. I jot the details down. I'm feeling efficient. I'm doing this like a job of work – keeping my emotions at bay.

In Marriages, I subtract nine months from my birth – January 1964 – and work back. I find nothing, so I widen the net and, finally, in a book I've scanned already, I find something I must have missed first time: Durrant, M. J. W. married de Bueger (my mother's maiden name: there is no lack of detail in my head about *her* life), Chelsea, September 1963.

Which leaves me with Deaths. This will be straightforward. There are photographs of me with him until I'm almost a year old: then they stop. I check the appropriate books. Nothing. I go earlier, right back to the month of my birth, in case I have it wrong. Then, hardly daring to believe I may have had more of him than I had thought, I go later. I go through every volume until 1967, when I would have been three years old. Nothing.

It's evading me. There's this big thing and I can't find it. I want to cry. I don't feel efficient any more, but muddled and flailing. All these names, all these deaths. Why can't I find a record of his? I am in Deaths for maybe an hour and in that time, his life expands and contracts.

There was a building site along from our house when I was growing up. It lay fallow for a couple of years and I'd hang out there with the willowherb and stray cats, staring up as the planes crossed over the sky. I used to imagine that one day I'd go home, wandering down the street in the half light, in the dusk, and I'd be some distance from the house when I'd see a man in uniform, in a hat, with a bag – a kind of grip – approaching our house. And he would stop when he saw me coming and frown slightly because it would be hard to see in the light, but then he'd put his bag down and his arms would open and that's when I would start to run.

This picture comes to me when I can't find a record of his death. But I'm older, and I know now that the image of the returning man came from a children's book called *The Lord of the Rushie River*, in which the father isn't a pilot, but a sailor, and the girl is looked after by swans. I know my father's dead. It's just the record that's missing.

It's hot in here and the shuffling and shunting seems not rhythmic and relaxing but oppressive. I decide to leave.

I'm at the tube when something else troubles me.

I lean against the wall and rummage for my notes. Their marriage: September 1963. I do my maths. I hadn't missed it first time; I hadn't checked that book before. They got married four months before I was born. My mother was pregnant! What a gift that should be for a daughter who is trying to place herself in the centre of the relationship, who wants, I realize, to put herself between them. But it's too sad for that. I thought they had had some time together, Malta, was it? Some story about water-skiing and a capsized speedboat and a camera that fell to the bottom of the Med. Scotland?

I retrace my steps. The birth date has also begun to niggle at me, too. I'd been assuming clerical error, but wouldn't you expect his full initials to be on his birth certificate?

The Family Records Centre has got busier. I check his birth first. In July 1935 I find a far more plausible entry with the full initials – M. J. W. Durrant (mother's maiden name: Morison) – born in Portsmouth. So I *had* got that wrong. Less haste. And in Marriages, I find I was mistaken here too. They didn't get married in September 1963, but September *1962*. I had just copied it down inaccurately in my notebook. I don't feel disappointed, but relieved. They had a bit of time, then. They married each other because they wanted to, not because my mother was pregnant.

At the desk I ask if they have special files for servicemen and women and discover they do, though the files are confusing and seem to end in 1965. I have to decide whether he died 'At Sea' or 'In the Air', though it turns out not to matter as he isn't filed in either. Back at the desk, I have a mini-altercation with the man who says that if my father flew planes, he would be filed under army. 'It's not the army; it's the navy,' I insist. 'The Fleet Air Arm is the flying wing of the navy. He was killed off the Dorset coast.'

'Abroad, then,' he says.

I tell him I don't think Lyme Bay counts as Abroad.

He says, 'Army or Abroad, that's the best I can do.'

I go back to the shelves, a little tearful, and there is a grey-haired man with a nice face, vying for the same files and I ask him if he knows where the post-1965 Abroad files are. We get to talking – he's an American and he's researching a shipwreck for a book. He was at the Fleet Air Arm Museum at Yeovilton only the week before. He says they should be able to show me my father's naval records. Another browsing military expert joins in and the two of them give me a potted guide, at a distance, of the relevant archives. I realize I'm hoping one of them is going to take me under their wing, offer to come with me, *to do it all for me*. I want to give this over to a nice comforting older man. This is a common instinct of mine that needs examining. But then the American says, 'Of course, if he was missing, they might not have given a death certificate for quite some time.'

'You mean, in case he came back?'

'In the US, it takes seven years,' he says. 'I don't know how long it takes here.'

We stare at the stacks of files. 'Isn't there anyone else you can ask?' he adds. 'I assume your mother's passed away?'

I tell him she lives two miles from me in London. 'Why don't you ask her?' he says. I explain about not wanting to upset her.

There's a pause. He says quietly, 'She might surprise you.'

*

Three weeks later and 35,000 troops have set off for the Gulf. The *Guardian* reports the 'flagship aircraft carrier' *Ark Royal* is at the head of a sixteen-ship flotilla. Eight hundred and fifty navy personnel are already there.

I'm on an early morning train from Clapham Junction to Yeovil Junction. The *Guardian* also says 'support for the war falls to a new low'. They've printed a poem by Harold Pinter in which he depicts the forces as 'blind idiots', 'pawns of government'. It was the same the previous day at the school gates. A mother said, 'You see those troops, and those ships, and those planes lining up and it makes you feel sick to the pit of your stomach.'

There is something going on here that is not just antipathy to this particular war. It's an alienation from the forces in general. And it would be so much easier to nod and smile, to feel distant not just from the war, but from those involved in it too, the sailors, the soldiers, their fathers and mothers, wives and children and husbands, waving them off at Portsmouth with their tight, anxious faces, their patriotic chants. Maybe a year ago I would have done. But I'm implicated now. If my father was alive, I could be one of them, frantically clutching my Union Jack at the water's edge. This makes me uncomfortable. I don't want to be on their side. I've started wishing he'd been a writer, or an artist, or a professional musician like his own father. *His* house was full of books and music. What was my father doing joining up?

I look away from the paper as the West Country streaks past. The landscape distracts me. My mother and I lived in Somerset, in a housing estate on the outskirts of a small village near Yeovilton (where my father had been stationed), until I was six. The soft colours and shapes – those curves, that roundness – of the land looks like home. When I cross the bridge at Yeovil Junction with its tarmacked slats through which you can see the rails beneath, I am five years old, come to pick up my grandparents.

I've made some steps forward since my trip to the Family Records Office. Sifting through my pile of photographs I found a small blue leaflet, the 'Register of Old Pangbournians (To March 1963)', which lists M. J. W. Durrant as 1949/53. Through the website Friends Reunited I've emailed all seven of the entries for 1953. Five replied. 'Greetings and nautical salutations' began one 'semi-retired, balding salt'. Another opens, 'VMT for your message'.

None professes to have known my father very well. He was 'of the exalted class' who joined the Royal rather than merchant navy, signing up through

Dartmouth Naval College in May 1953. He was a 'shorter in height cadet', 'very good at sailing and a thoroughly nice person'. Someone had looked him up in 'The Log, no 98' and could tell me that he was in form VI DE, gained a prize in open navigation in 1952, was secretary of the photographical society and 'a stalwart of sabre'. Another correspondent, who had gone on from school to Dartmouth with him and touchingly, *excitingly* referred to 'Mike' (as in my email I hadn't), reported that there was a reunion of their entry term coming up and he would contact all seventy names on the list.

I've received one email as a result that fills me with expectation. It's from a Mike Buchanan, who was in 'T group sub-lieutenants doing courses from September 1956–57'. His memory of Mike is of 'a quiet, reserved, but extremely courteous and pleasant colleague'. He remembers going to a ball with him on Whale Island (part of the naval base) at Christmas 1956, and that the two of them and their girlfriends spent the night at my grandfather's house in Old Portsmouth. 'I also recall that after the ball we all went out to Bishop Waltham, to the house of Simon Thomas's girlfriend and were stranded there by a pea fog preventing our return until the following morning.' He has passed on my details to Commander A.

W. Stewart Fitzroy who, he says, knew my father very well, and attaches a group photograph from his archives. There are fourteen men in the line-up, as well as my father, with side-combed hair, in a jacket that's too large. He has named them all. (Four of them are called Mike; I've learnt there are a lot of Mikes in the navy.) Six of them were subsequently killed, including the fellow-ball-goer, Simon Thomas, father of the actress Kristin Scott Thomas, who is sitting next to my father and who died in an identical accident to him, a few weeks before. They were both flying a plane called a Sea Vixen.

I had long assumed that the MoD – that closed shop, full of secrets and self-protection – would stonewall me if I contacted them for information. And I have received notification from them that my father's naval record would only be available to me on receipt of a death certificate and the permission of the next of kin (my mother). For the moment, I have neither.

It is a different matter at the Fleet Air Arm Museum. Gerry Spence, the man who had answered the phone, couldn't have been more chatty. I needed to speak to Jan – 'Janet but she never uses it' – who was off skiing ('lucky girl'). When I gave him my father's name and told him he flew Sea Vixens, he said, 'I'm getting a vibe here. I've seen this one before.'

He told me during our phone conversation that the Sea Vixen had been a revolutionary plane in the early sixties, the first naval supersonic night fighter. It had nuclear capability. He also called the early sixties 'a rather shameful period in naval history, a period in which we lost an awful lot of aircrew. An awful lot of Sea Vixen crew in particular were killed.' The sixties, *peacetime*. Technology, he explained, was racing ahead; it was the height of the Cold War. Russia was the enemy. Ammunition was being tested. People were pushed, 'training and safety didn't keep up'. About eighteen months before my call, there had been a reunion for Sea Vixen pilots and a number of daughters and sons had been there trying to find out about their fathers, just like me. A whole load of them. A whole load of non-combative Sea Vixen deaths. He thinks someone called Nobby Hall might have been charged with compiling a report on this. My father was unlucky, he said. By 1965 things had improved.

I looked Sea Vixens up on Google while he was talking. One sentence leapt out: 'A risk to aircrew never before experienced.'

I made an appointment to see Jan. 'Anything we've

got on your old man,' said Gerry Spence (my *old
man*?), 'you can have.'

Yeovilton airbase was rebuilt in 2001, but the road
through it is unchanged: it's straight, lined with small
trees and stunted street lamps. Driving along it in the
back of the taxi I get another strong recollection. We
used to come here for Air Day, every August, though
the memory is murky. I have a feeling it was an annual
outing that my mother hated.

The museum and archive is in a huge hanger. It
has real planes in here. I overhear someone ask direc-
tions to the loo: 'Cross the warehouse,' they're told,
'and turn left at Concorde's wing'. Waiting for Jan, I
search the shop for a Sea Vixen model kit. There is
only one left. When Jan arrives, I point this out and
she says, 'Yes. Bit of a hole on the Sea Vixen. It's something we're trying to sort out.' All the kits, she says, are
now made in Russia. I wonder what my father would
have thought of that.

We go through the museum to reach the archive. I
have the impression she's dallying, playing for time.
It's hard to talk over the simulated take off of the Hur-
ricane on the screen at one end. She says something
about 'the sensitivity of some of the material' she's

turned up. 'There's a bit of a black hole on some of his life,' she shouts. All these holes. I feel as though I'm being given a government health warning.

We stop at a plane. It's huge. You have to look up at its underbelly. There is a tiny window at the tip, and then a vast hulking, streaming expanse of grey metal. You'd need a ladder to see in. Jan tells me it's a Sea Vixen.

The worst thing about them, she shouts above the screaming of the simulated take-off, apart from their unprecedented power and size, was the position of the observer. He was seated lower than the pilot, and they used to have to blackout his window so the instruments would show up. They'd fly blind, dependent on the pilot for his eyes. 'Observers hated the Sea Vixen,' she yells.

I hadn't thought about my father's observer until this moment. There was a boy of my age I used to play with called Simon Sutton. His mother remarried much faster than mine. There was a jolly man he called 'Dad' but I don't think it was his real one. His real father was my father's observer. My father was 'his eyes'. I am filled with a terrible sense of foreboding.

I say, 'There were a lot of accidents on Sea Vixens, weren't there?' and she says yes. 'They must have been very dangerous,' I say.

She looks away. 'Your father's accident wasn't to do with the plane,' she says.

I've got my notebook out. I am in full businesslike journalistic mode. But for the moment, I can't bring myself to ask any more.

The archive itself is a shabby rabbit warren of windowless rooms. There are signs on desks saying things like, 'Would you like to speak to the man in charge of the women who know what's happening?' Jan leads me into an empty cubicle with its own door. On the table lies a pile of large books. She has put together what she can find on my father's naval career; these are the records of the ships and squadrons he was in. Here is evidence of his life, from his early days as a cadet on HMS *Triumph*, to a midshipman on HMS *Gambia*, through flying and navigation courses, to sub-lieutenant to lieutenant in 766 Squadron and 892, and 750, 764, 890, attached to HMS *Victorious* and *Ark Royal* and *Fulmar* and *Heron* . . . to his final role, after his training at Whale Island, Portsmouth – on what she calls the 'Ssssh Bomb Course' – as air weapons instructor. He missed Korea and Vietnam, only skirted Suez, but he was active enough. He travelled to Africa, the Far East, to Ceylon, Singapore, Mombassa, Majorca, Malta. There is death in these records ('the search following last night's accident was abandoned at 10.00'), political tension ('trouble is brewing in Kuwait'); and parties ('S-Lt Sutton celebrated his twenty-first birthday by inviting the squadron officers to join him in a glass of very potent punch'). In the 1950s, people didn't travel like they do now. My father, at least, saw the world. It's a life *seen*. I start to read more thoroughly, writing notes ('19 Sep, 61: 'Durrant escaped with cuts to his flying overalls when the canopy of X5604 shattered at 40,000 feet'), jotting down the names of men who worked and flew along-side him (several of them with the same names as widows my mother knows) while Jan flutters in and out, checking I'm OK.

At one point, I look up to ask her what she thought it felt like to be a pilot on an aircraft carrier, whether you felt out of place among all those sailors, or a mem-ber of an elite? And she calls in David Hobbs, the head curator, a former pilot himself. He has a lot to say. He perches on the edge of the table and pours forth about how the Fleet Air Arm was known as the 'Branch', submariners were called the 'Trade' and smelt of engine oil and cabbage. How the RAF were considered 'jobsworths', while the FAA would do 'any-thing asked of us'. He talks about the Cold War, the responsibility men like my father would have felt to fend off the 'big Russian bear', to 'defend the

Commonwealth', how joining the navy was like joining the Firm, how it all changed with the cuts of 1966
– 'after your father's time of course'. I'm smiling and
listening, but at the same time my eyes keep being
drawn back to the treasure trove in front of me. I'm
still searching the pages. And then I see it.

It's a photograph. It's of only four men, standing
casually, in flying suits. One of them is my father.
Maybe I haven't seen photographs of him at this age
before. But there is something about the eyes, the eyebrows, the chubbiness of the cheeks – they're the
features of my youngest son. It's like looking at Joe.
And the feeling I get – a terrible, heartbreaking pang
of tenderness – is so strong I find I've put my hand to
my mouth.

I don't think Jan can have noticed this because it's
then that she says, 'Maybe this would be a good time
to show you his incident report, and maybe David,
while you're here, you could explain?' She is fiddling
nervously with a piece of card, and he starts telling me
about the manoeuvre my father was doing the night
he died.

I drag my eyes away from the picture and try to
concentrate. It involved something called a Lepus
flare. There were three planes, and a ship called HMS
Murray. The planes were dropping bombs, just off

Portland Bill, and, in order to drop the bombs, they needed to illuminate the target – in this case an area to one side of the ship – first. They would fly in very fast, 'doing aeronautical display stuff', do a hard turn, drop the Lepus flare (powerful enough to be a sort of bomb itself), twist, angle, return and drop the real bomb, in theory before the target had a chance to respond. My father was the third plane. 'It was night. It was November,' David Hobbs says. 'Visibility over the sea would have been very poor. Non-existent. We know what happens to the canals in the ear doing aeronautical manoeuvres. It's like vertigo. You see the instrument panel spinning – you're rolling and pulling about 5G – about five times your body weight. You don't trust your eyes. Instruments have been known to go wrong . . .' Jan holds out the piece of card in her hand. It's the incident report. 'Pilot disorientation,' she says, 'is very common.'

David says, 'We don't know this for sure. There were no witnesses, no sign of the plane. They didn't have sonar technology. The wreckage would still be at the bottom there. It's just the most likely scenario.'

I take the card, and write down what it says: 'Considered probably due to disorientation, possibly due to aircraft malfunction or some other distraction to the pilot during the manoeuvre.' The date is 25.11.64.

Pilot: Lt M. J. W. Durrant (killed). Aircrew: Lt B. A. Last (killed).

David starts telling a story about a friend of his who was flying a Sea Vixen at night, off Singapore, and felt a bump while turning for a climb, and thought he'd hit a bird. It was only when he got back to the ship that he realized he'd hit the water. He'd flown down, not up. His calculations were miles out. Gerry Spence, my friend from the phone, shambles in and tells David about the Sea Vixen he saw crash 'just off the base'. They talk among themselves about how hard deck-landings could be with Sea Vixens, how it flew 'on the margins of stability'. Jan goes to get a sample list of Sea Vixen accidents. The three of them study it. There are fifty-two individual tragedies on a single page ('lost at sea'; 'crashed on launch'; 'missing from a sortie'). 'The Sea Vixen,' David Hobbs says, 'was, how shall I put it, somewhat unforgiving.' I'm still writing. I still don't look up.

After a bit, I realize I can't see the words any more. Jan puts a box of tissues next to me. They're decorated with cartoon cats. I stop writing. I stare at the page. David says, 'They wouldn't have known a thing. They wouldn't have known what hit them.' But they don't understand. I'm still crying about the picture, for the boy in his twenties who looks like my Joe, the grandson he never knew.

Over the next few weeks, emails and letters start flooding in. You could argue I've timed my research well. These men are retired now, bored, nostalgic. But I'm overwhelmed by their kindness. Some of them scour their attics, find photographs – of schoolboys in ridiculously over-large military uniform, of midshipmen in shorts fiddling about with motorboats, of naval officers, off-duty in white shirts and ties, hitting Hong Kong – that they copy and send. Some rifle through their shelves for books I might find useful; one surrenders his whole navy archive, after asking his daughter if she minds it being passed on to someone else's.

I talk to a lot of sixty-eight-year-old men. I have tea with a former pilot who left the navy in 1963 but still lives within a few miles of the airbase, who tells me, 'We're a clan; and you're one of us now.' I chat to a retired submariner who says Mike was 'bloody awful at astro-navigation', and recounts how the death of a contemporary was such a frequent occurrence, 'You went to the funeral and I wouldn't say you didn't feel it, but . . .' He breaks off and his voice changes. 'I have more time to reflect now. Looking back, each and every one of them was an awful accident.' And I meet the commander, A. W. Stewart Fitzroy – Algy – in a wine bar off the Strand. 'To be honest,' he says, 'I didn't know he'd married, let alone sprogged.' But he tells me about the early days he spent touring the Commonwealth with Mike in HMS *Gambia* and HMS *Triumph*, the encounters with Emperor Haile Selassie and his grandson Alexander Testor, who trained alongside them for a while before returning to Ethiopia where he 'personally beheaded eight mutineers'; the slung hammocks you slept in, the rats in the pipes overhead, the Italian girls you picked up, the young colonial fillies you tried your arm with. In Ceylon, they travelled to Kandy to ride elephants and Algy wanted to find a relative, who was a tea-planter. No one, including Mike, would come with him. 'They didn't want to go into black man's country,' he says. He catches my expression. 'We were all racist then,' he adds. 'That's what it was like.'

When I began all this, I set out to learn about a wonderful man. The anecdote about 'black man's country' would have appalled me. I do pause when I hear it and I think quite a lot about it afterwards, but I know we are talking about different times and I know, too, that truth has come to matter to me most.

I have also begun to feel a certain distance from my subject. I grip my notebook and scribble with my pen so hard that sometimes my interviewees, in the stream of some personal anecdote, look puzzled and ask me to put it down. But I'm collecting information. Not just anecdotes, but navy parlance. I discover that 'dog-robbers' are 'relaxed rig', that anyone with the surname White is called Chalky, that a cup of tea is 'a wet', biscuits are 'hard tack', that a trip to the pub, even if you're already on land, is a 'run ashore' and that, generally in service life, you run up against a hell of a lot of 'wimps' and even more 'absolute prats'.

I also absorb a lot about these men. Quite often, we talk a little bit about my father, and a great deal about them. Memory, after all, fades. Forty years is a long time. Someone who might have been a close friend of his between 1950 and 1955 – one of the few best friends to fit into my father's own life – has had a great many more close friends since. If I'd asked *him* about *them* he might have called them his best muckers, but all these years later he's only someone they vaguely knew. There are things I learn, but the information comes at arm's length, filtered. I have a disquieting phone conversation with Sir Michael Layard, the Second Sea Lord, a contemporary of my father in the navy and at school who, I'd been told, was part of the search party the night of his accident. He came to the phone from the garden, where he was repainting his fence, pottering about as men of that age do. He was full of charm, 'delighted' to talk about my 'dear, departed old dad', rapt with some anecdote about his own no-show at my christening. On my father's accident, which he didn't remember *as such*, he told me, 'When you rolled off the top of your loop and turned back to the target from pitch darkness to blinding light, the chances of controlling your aircraft were almost zero.' But when I suggested that no one should have been asked to do such an exercise, he answered smoothly, 'It's pointless to conjecture on the cause. These things happen.' Well, maybe they shouldn't, I want to scream, but I don't.

At moments like this I'm filled with anger. I think, why are you alive and he isn't? At other times, talking to a retired pilot in a room filled with photographs of family and dogs, I wonder more benignly if he'd be like them, pootling around in boats, complaining about his sons-in-law, propping up the bar at the golf club, repainting his fence. I want to know about their daughters and what they're up to (married mostly, marvellous mothers). I wonder if my life would be like theirs if he hadn't died. If we hadn't moved to London, if my mother hadn't gone back out to work, if I hadn't spent my early years surrounded by women . . . It occurs to me for the first time that much of what I like about my life has come about because he *did* die. Whatever the surface may suggest, I never think of myself, deep down, as conventional. And it's terrible to admit it, because of the circumstances that brought it about, but I like it that way.

And then occasionally, something gut-wrenching happens, when I lose all composure. At the Fleet Air Arm Museum I jotted down any names that cropped up more than once in connection with Lt M. J. W. Durrant. I then cross-referenced these to a phone directory of current Fleet Air Arm members, and came up with a list of about twenty still living, whom I then set about ringing. I began to feel foolish after seven or eight had racked their memories to put a face to the name and had almost given up when, one evening, I phone someone called Geoff Courtis who, a cocky-looking lad with a wicked grin, is sitting next to my father in several of the photographs sent to me by other people. A woman answers. She asks, with a slight note of suspicion, if I'd like to leave a message for her husband, and I find myself giving the whole spiel.

There is a long silence. Then she says, 'But Mike was our best man.'

I can't quite describe what this makes me feel. It's like a proof of something. I've been thinking so much of him as an absence, and then suddenly he's important, he's in the middle of someone's life, he meant enough to them to be best man at their wedding. When Geoff Courtis rings back, I find his voice the nicest I've ever heard. He says after a while, 'Sorry, I haven't thought about him for years and now, well . . .' His voice cracks with emotion. He can't find the right words. It's as close to my father as I'm going to get, I think. I have this picture in front of me of Geoff as a young man, his shoulder touching my father's and I want to talk to him all night. I don't want him to hang up.

There's another deeply moving encounter to come. Jan at the Fleet Air Arm Museum had worked out there was an observer called Graham Wilcock I should meet. I recognized the name immediately. He was someone we used to see, in our old life, before my mother remarried. That the connection was my father was something I'd never grasped. I wrote to him and took the train down to Somerset to see him.

'I'll get a taxi from the station,' I said.

'You damn well will not,' he answered.

When I get off the train, I see a grey bearded middle-aged man waiting at the end of the platform.

His face, as it gets clearer, is like a familiar map, even though I probably haven't seen him since I was twelve. When I get up to him, he says, 'That's Mike Durrant's daughter all right,' and then we're both so choked up we don't say any more all the way to the car.

We sit in his sitting room and all afternoon he talks me through my father's life. I say, 'I might cry but ignore me.' He says, 'Same applies to me.' He gets out his albums, and his logbook. I hear about the near-misses, the seat-of-the-pants stuff, the day they landed at Yeovilton in a thunderstorm, how there was a total electrical failure. 'You're doing 130 knots, a mile of wet concrete, no lights, driving rain and wind; we aquaplaned, yawed around, he wasn't in control. I didn't dare say a word and then at the far end of the runway there was an arrester wire; he put the deck hook down and we caught it. I didn't believe the compass in front of me. I said, "Which way are we pointing?" He said, "Have we stopped?"'

Another time, flying back to Yeovilton from the Far East, they were just south of Sardinia – almost home – when they got a call from the plane in front saying their instruments were out and they needed guiding in. Thick layers of cloud, took half an hour to find him ('a terrible Saturday afternoon in December'), and then when they reached the airbase, the main landing strip was taken and the chap they guided in took the second and there was some cock-up on that and Mike and he had to stay up in the sky for ages, running out of fuel. It got so bad, Mike said they really ought to head off to Lyme Bay – 'ditch the plane and bail out' – but they had all their Singapore Christmas goodies and booze on board, 'so we were buggered if we were going to do that.' In the end, they came in on the back of the other chap, 'and, in fact, it was easy to stop in time because the plane was so light – there was no fuel left.'

I get a sense of how much my father loved flying, the thrill of it, the camaraderie, the beauty – the ethereal colours of St Elmo's Fire, the first time you flew supersonic, the smoke ring you saw from the shockwave. I stare at the handsome man in the pictures Graham shows me. I think I'm falling in love with him.

Sometimes Graham has to stop, and at the end of the day he looks drained. He was at sea when he heard the news. He rang his wife and she went straight to my mother's . . . I show him the final incident report. He points out the 'probably' and the 'possibly' in its conclusions. I've started crying now.

He waits a while, then shakes his head. 'I'd have done anything, flown anywhere, with him.'

When I finally leave, he suggests more people I should ring. One of them, Dave Henry, was the co-ordinator on board the ship HMS *Murray*, which was positioned just off Portland Bill the night my father died. I phone him a few days later and catch him as he's on his way out to mow the bowling green. He remembers the night in question very well. He was listening on the radio as the exercise took place. The first two planes came in and went. 'Then the third plane – your father's. We heard the call of his aircraft delivering, "Bomb dropped." But we never saw the bomb. We saw nothing.' Wouldn't he have *heard* something if that was the moment the plane crashed?

'I've seen three of those aircraft going into the water,' he replies. 'Sometimes you hear absolutely nothing. It's a question of how they hit the water. It can be silent.'

Within an hour of what he'd assumed was a simple 'hang up' – what you call it when a bomb doesn't go off – Henry got a message back from Yeovilton to say only two aircraft had been recovered. 'We went into search mode all night. The search continued all the next day. I spent it on the bridge. The least I can do, I thought, was *see something*. We didn't find anything.

The Lepus flare was the most difficult bloomin' thing we ever did. To be honest, it was the device they'd developed for the nuclear weapon. It wasn't a flare or a rocket. To power that sort of illumination, it had to be a pure bomb. The timing was vital. It's not defensible when you look back, this sort of thing. But it was what happened. We didn't think about it then.'

A few days after this, I start losing the baby I'm carrying. I ring my mother to tell her and she comes round. Her husband is with her. Maybe if you're widowed at twenty-nine, you never want to be separated from a husband again. But I'm surprised. I want to cry with her and be comforted, but we don't talk about the miscarriage. We behave as if nothing is happening. We talk about the congestion charge, what they've seen at the theatre. My visit to Graham and Eileen Wilcock is on the tip of my tongue. But I don't tell her. I protect it. My father belongs to me now. We drink tea while I bleed, while the hope of any life inside me is sapped away, and after a while I say brightly, 'Whatever happened to Simon Sutton? What's he up to?' and she tells me he lives in Chiswick. 'Computers I think,' she says. Not telling her, I realize, isn't kindness. It's an act of aggression.

I need a little time to adjust to the loss of my baby before I feel ready to return to the loss of my father, but when I'm better, I go to the library and look Simon Sutton up in the Chiswick directory and there he is: Simon Last-Sutton, a phone number and an address. The 'Last' – the addition of his real father's surname – is a clue to something. I write him a letter, explaining 'my search' and asking if he'd like to get in touch.

It's an odd spring. Cheek-numbingly cold days follow days that are almost sultry in their warmth. From my desk, I watch the blossom come out on the cherry tree by the window; one morning the boughs bask, the next the flowers are sodden, buffeted to the pavement by wild wind. I find a drowning bee in an empty pot in the garden. I think he's already dead, but his legs move when I pour the water out. Another day, I rescue an early cabbage white from the skylight in the kitchen.

They are months in which I gain and I lose. There are days when I am filled with well-being. The affection provoked in me by some of the people I talk to is almost erotic in its strength. I find out more about my father than I imagined possible. I drink it in. I fall in love with what I discover. And yet even at the height of my excitement, the immediacy, and the *closeness* to him I feel when I flesh out a new fact, can leave a terrible sense of loss. I feel like I'm getting there, that any minute I'm going to find him, I'm going to *have* him, and I have to force myself to remember that this is it. The facts, the stories, the conversations are all there is. I'm not going to turn a corner and find him standing in his uniform, holding his hat, outside our old house.

Other things happen. Bill Peppe contacts me from the Isle of Skye to say that in the charity auction subsequent to my father's death (in which non-personal possessions were sold over the odds for the sake of his widow), he bought his flying grip, that he still has it – initialled – and I can collect it anytime. I plan to go and get it over the summer. And my father's birth certificate arrives. I discover, finally, that the J stands for John, the W for Wavell and that he was born at home on 11 July 1935 at 319 Hawthorn Crescent, Cosham, in the district of Portsmouth. His mother's name was Elizabeth Adelaide Bellechasse Durrant, formerly Morison.

I muse on this grandmother whom I never knew, the same blood relationship to me as my beloved maternal granny, but whom I never think about. Somewhere, there's a gravestone unattended, which seems awful as I've often wished that my father had a gravestone, that there was somewhere to *go*. I wonder if he ever went, if he would cry there and wish for her and imagine her coming back. I vow to return to the Family Records Centre and find out more about her. It strikes me that I don't even know how old my father was when *she* died. I think again about my sons. The thought of them losing either me or their father is unbearable.

But I also track down another grandmother, one I've never met, a step-grandmother, my grandfather's third wife – who tells me about a charming, sulky boy, damaged by his first stepmother, flirtatious and delighted with the second, to be resentful of the third. He joined the navy, she thinks, to rebel against the artistic surroundings in which he grew up. 'He was moody and insecure – powerful deep waters,' she tells me. 'But he had a smile that lit up his face.'

I discover something else, too, that at six he had been sent by his father and stepmother number one to a boarding school on the Isle of Wight. The school was called Little Appley and by a strange stroke of serendipity it turns out to be less than a mile from Seaview, a village where I've been going for holidays for the last twenty years. I'm there at Easter and I pass the house – now a hotel called Appley Manor with orange spangled carpets and a carvery in the bar – and draw up outside with the children. A chatty waiter shows us round. The headmaster's office is the dining room; the dormitory has been divided into rooms with flimsy four-posters. The school, if his memory's not mistaken, was run by a retired naval captain: 'Cold showers, beatings. That sort of thing.' In the grounds are fruit trees and a disused swimming pool, edged by brambles and barbed wire. My eldest, Barney, wants to explore. He's only six. I hold him tight.

When we get back, there's a phone call from Simon Last-Sutton. He's been away; he's rung the moment he got my letter. My 'quest', as he puts it, has coincided with one of his own. We arrange to meet almost immediately in Shepherd's Market in central London.

For most of my research I have been assiduous in my note-taking, and not simply as a distraction from tears or as a distancing technique. It's as if by getting it all down in ink I will be left with something life-size. But I don't write notes when I meet Simon. And afterwards, when I think back about the afternoon, the facts that we build together of our fathers' lives and deaths sink like silt. The two of us have little in common – but at the same time we have everything. We begin embarrassed, end awkward, but in the middle is a conversation of rare intimacy. I recognize in what he says certain things that, until now, underpinned my own life. There is the same hero-worship of his father and his kind ('the formula-one boys of the navy'), the same irrational anger towards his mother, whom he can't forgive for selling his father's uniform. He grew up with the same fantasy that his father had been shot down on the Russian border and was out there, alive, just waiting to come back. He shares my new fury at what they were expected to do: 'The Sea Vixen was a flying coffin'; the sense of conspiracy at the absence of evidence: 'There were ships in Lyme Bay, a fishing fleet on its way back in, submarines mucking about in the water. I can't believe no one saw anything.' He says he wants his own ashes scattered in Lyme Bay, 'so that my dad and I will be together', and it isn't just that it's startling to hear someone voice my own thoughts, but that I see them for a moment more objectively: the poignant absurdity of a grown man and woman with partners and in my case children, wanting to be buried with a parent.

Something happens after my meeting with Simon. It is partly that I still want to see a death certificate, which my mother must have had in order to remarry; partly that hearing him talk about his existing parent puts my feelings about my own in relief. I wonder if I haven't been childish, if it isn't time to grow up. And one day, shortly after this, I'm helping my mother decide what to wear to a cousin's wedding and I hear myself say, casually almost, 'By the way, I've been finding out a bit about Mike.' (I can say his name after all.) She doesn't say much at the time. She looks at me oddly and says, 'Oh I'm glad,' as if she's been *waiting* for me to do it. But a few days later she comes round with the death certificate (issued on 26 January 1965, not seven years but two months after he died), and the tears that I may have been dreading all along run down her face and she starts talking about their marriage and how they met (on leave in London, he rang the flat where she lived in search of a girl who'd stayed there months before; her flatmate invited him round anyway . . . a coffee, a drink, a ball, engaged in two weeks!) and their life together in Malta and Scotland. She said after his own unhappy childhood he'd been wary of family life, but that embarking upon one of his own had made him happier than he'd ever imagined.

She cries most painfully when she talks, not about the night he didn't come home, but about the summer just before – a new baby, a new kitten, a new house, and him off, without any notice, to Singapore (part of a show of force against Sukarno, who in '64 was barring British ships from international waters: I know that now from reading the records), 'with no sign when they'd let him back'. The baby cried all the time, the cat kept disappearing. She wrote to him telling

him she didn't mind what he did, he could be a milkman for all she cared, but she wanted him out of the
navy, and home.

I don't say anything, but I know that he had two
families and that she and I may have been one of
them, but that the navy, from the age of six, had been
the other.

She's been reading some letters she hasn't read for
years and, when she's wiped her eyes, she starts telling
stories I've never heard before. The Nina and Fred-
erick record they listened to all night when they were
courting; the time after they were married when his
plane kept buzzing her ferry from Malta to Naples;
the fact he wore a sarong not pyjamas. She says she'll
think about whether to let me read these letters. She's
diffident and I think perhaps she's not going to – that
perhaps after this moment of light he won't be mentioned again – but the next time she comes, she's
carrying an Ottakar's plastic bag. Letters he's written
to her. Love letters. His own words. His own thoughts.
She puts the bag on the hall table and we go into the
kitchen. She's twitchy. She keeps looking around herself. At one point, she says, 'Oh God, where have I put
the letters?'

When she leaves, we put them in a safe place, high

on a bookshelf, out of harm's way. I can have more, she says, when I've read those.

They are still there, in their bag. At the beginning of all this, I would have torn off the envelopes, scoured them, worked my way through, absorbed each one, drunk in every word for myself. But they sit there, out of reach from the children, out of reach from me.

I opened one and found the intimacy of it overwhelming. Maybe I should leave the contents to her. I know there is a lot more to find out about my father. But I know where to look now. I know there are books with his name in, where you can trace things that happened. I know a little boy where you can trace some of the features of his face. I know there are people who remember him, who will still cry when they think too hard about him. I know that one of them is my mother. And that I only have to ask.

The other day I told an old friend what I'd been up to and she said, 'Oh yes, I remember you had a jumper of your dad's. Do you still have it?' I told her I did.

Blackpool Summer
William Fiennes

After my final exams at university I took a summer job
on the games stalls in Blackpool. My brother worked
for a leisure business running amusement arcades
and fairground concessions in seaside resorts, and
that summer he was in charge of the Blackpool operation. Most of my friends were embarking on careers,
but I didn't know what I wanted to do; I couldn't see
the outline of the life I belonged in. I'd never been to
Blackpool. I imagined noise and colour and light,
a funfair vividness. When Martin mentioned he was
recruiting people for the season, I said yes without
thinking.

The summer staff gathered like a tribe. We wore
red short-sleeved 'First Prize Games' polo shirts and
matching nylon bomber jackets, navy-blue waiters'
pouches of float change slung round our waists. Nick,
Jon, Anna, Richard and Michelle were students at Liverpool and Leeds; Big John weighed eighteen stone;

Blackpool Summer

Jimmy came from Birkenhead and had a place at drama school; Ralph was in his forties and had a finger missing; Sharon dotted her *i*s with capacious hearts. Some lived in Blackpool; most lived outside, catching the bus in from Lytham St Annes, Poulton-le-Fylde, Wrea Green and Freckleton. We took turns on Central Pier and North Pier and in the Tower, looking after the Milk Can, Basketball Shoot, Lotta Bottle, Crossbow, Test-Your-Strength and Wiggle Wire; we met in pubs after work, flipping beer mats off the table edges and catching them mid-spin; we queued at the roped entrances to basement nightclubs, voices hoarse from ten-hour shifts on the stalls.

I walked miles each day along the seafront to and from the piers and the Tower. I grew familiar with loose canvas flags in deckchair frames, shambling donkeys on the broad sands, the liquid electronic trills and scales of fruit machines and video games, the Big Wheel on Central Pier, the lights of the Pleasure Beach, the Tower's stubby Eiffel-like girder-work, gypsy fortune-teller cabins, girls in green striped pinafores wrapping sticks of Blackpool Rock in cellophane, the pram-bustle on the esplanade, the trams going back and forth to Fleetwood, Cleveleys, Bispham and Stargate. The work was dispiriting: the stream of people never let up; you could feel the growing marsupial weight of coins in the pouch at your waist; there was a market-boy patter and spiel we all fell into and hated ourselves for; you felt cynical catching someone's eye and taking their money without giving them a prize in return. The games were difficult, but they weren't fixed, and each day we'd hand over dozens of Kermits, Tiggers, Ninja Turtles and Tasmanian Dizzy Devils. Children got a helium balloon as well as a fluffy toy; sometimes you'd see clusters of our balloons like a wartime barrage floating above the crowds; we took gulps straight from the helium canister for the fun of our grass-blade cartoon voices.

Central Pier had the Big Wheel, a Waltzer, a rink of Dodgems and a public-address system that played the same selection of seventies rock classics over and over again: Slade, T. Rex, the Bay City Rollers. I knew when to rev along to the motorbike *vroom vroom* in 'Leader of the Pack', but the only song I looked forward to was Rod Stewart's 'Maggie May', especially the last minute or so when the mandolin comes in with its lovely repeating figure. We had a Test-Your-Strength machine close to the Big Wheel, and after a few days I had the technique down pat: it was about letting the sledgehammer gather its own strength on a quick, full, circular swing and hitting the button cleanly – then the steel marker would shoot up the rail and strike the bell with a loud *ding* that couldn't fail to invigorate your self-esteem, as if you'd sounded the note of your own presence in the world.

Every day a dwarf came to hang out on the pier. He was in his twenties; he wore a gold earring, jeans and a matching denim jacket. I never discovered his name, because everyone called him The Dwarf, or just Dwarf, even to his face; he didn't seem to mind. His friend owned the Waltzer – flame-licked booths spinning on their own axes as they orbited the control desk at the centre, the dwarf and his friend riding the troughs and swells between them like surfers, sometimes grabbing the rim of a booth and spinning it unforgivingly, grinning through the screams and curses. One night they took me to the *Page Three Stunnas!* show on the pier. The dwarf stood on a chair to watch the routines; much later I saw him sitting on a tall speaker-stack, kissing a dark-haired girl: she was standing; the dwarf's high perch brought their faces level, his palms flat in the small of her back, pieces of light reeling off the mirrorball.

Martin was ten years older than me; I looked up to him; I wanted his dynamism and self-possession, his ease and confidence with women. For a while he had a girlfriend in London, and sometimes they'd catch late trains and meet at Crewe station, stay in a hotel and be back at work by eight the next morning. Then the girl who cut his hair came to meet us for a drink and I saw Martin and Tracy holding hands under the table, and one night in a club a singer called Marilena told me how attractive she thought Martin was, and an hour later I glimpsed them through a crowd of dancers, leaning into each other, the red of my brother's 'First Prize Games' polo shirt, Marilena's arms around it. I'd been ill for two years, and somehow it had turned me in on myself; I was inhibited and self-conscious; I felt graceless. However much I loved Martin, however much we laughed and gossiped together, I looked on at his swashbuckling romantic life with a pang of loneliness, as if it were something withheld from me.

He had a one-bedroom flat in Naventi Court, two streets back from the seafront. Mike Nolan, one of the singers from Bucks Fizz, was renting a flat down the corridor. I used to pass him on his way to the basement gym, in a singlet and black lycra cycling shorts, gold streaks in his hair gleaming in the striplights. I slept on the sofa in the living room. The previous tenant had left a can of Mace 10% Pepper Spray on the hallway shelf; there were songs – Elvis Costello's 'I Want You'; John Martyn's 'Solid Air' – we played over and over and sang together; chemicals leaked from the tubing of the fridge-freezer, filling the flat with toxic fumes: we didn't go near the kitchenette for several days. We had full English breakfasts in the Piccadilly Tea Rooms; we ate chicken korma and lamb jalfrezi microwave ready meals in front of late-night highlights from the Barcelona Olympics: an archer lit an arrow with the Olympic flame, then loosed it on a long, high arc to fire the bowl of oil and start the games. One night, in the 400-metre semi-final, we saw the British runner Derek Redmond fall without warning in the fifth lane, his right hamstring gone. But he didn't lie there; he got to his feet again and hobbled on; he was determined to cross the finish line though all the other runners were far ahead. Suddenly, an older man was climbing over the advertising hoardings and running out onto the track towards Redmond. For a moment the commentators were confused, but then you saw that Redmond himself wasn't worried; in fact he'd put his arm round the older man's neck for support, and his father had his arm round his son's waist and was helping him on, and together they completed the lap and finished the race, embracing. I looked at Martin; his face was streaming. Mine was, too.

We had three stalls in Blackpool Tower, in a hall-

way between the Hornpipe Galley food court and
Jungle Jim's indoor adventure playground: rope
bridges, snake slides, ball swamps. During slow per-
iods I'd slip into one of the balconies overlooking the
Tower Ballroom – an opera-house luxuriance of deep
red upholstery and gilded plasterwork, a chandelier
twinkling over the sprung dance floor – and watch the
Mighty Wurlitzer organ rise out of the stage on a slow
hydraulic lift, the resident organist Phil Kelsall rising
with it like a ritzy sea-god from the depths, left hand
on the tiered keyboard, right hand waving like his
own metronome, the words 'BID ME DISCOURSE AND I
WILL LEND THEE MINE EARS' spelled out in gold letters
across the proscenium. Ballroom sessions began at
eleven o'clock in the morning; you'd see widows dancing brooch-to-brooch, leaning into waltz, foxtrot,
quickstep and cha-cha, mouthing the words to 'Moon
River' or 'April in Paris' or 'Let Me Call You Sweetheart'. But more often I'd work on North Pier, which
was as spacious and dignified as Central Pier was clut-
tered and raucous. There was an elegant small train
you could ride to the attractions at the far end: the
Carousel, the glassed-in Sun Lounge, and the North
Pier Theatre where the *Russ Abbot Show* played
nightly. Each afternoon, Russ would stride briskly
along the pier in a pulled-down baseball cap, hunch-

shouldered, hands thrust deep into his pockets as if it were the coldest day of the year, his sidekick Bella Emberg sauntering behind, smiling and signing autographs. A few minutes later, one of us would spot Russ's three dancers, the Russettes, heading in our direction, and we'd fight to have charge of the Basketball Shoot, which was right beside the stage door and so provided the best chance of heated metropolitan glances from Dominique, Theresa or Lizelle.

There was a helicopter pad at the end of North Pier, and sometimes celebrities flew in and walked past our games towards the town. One day the singer Lisa Stansfield arrived, and marched down the pier in the midst of an entourage. She wore a black trouser suit; her black hair had a polished enamel sheen.

'Lisa!' I shouted. 'Three for a pound, Lisa! You know you want to, Lisa!'

But she didn't even look; she just kept walking. Later in the season, the comedian Jim Davidson stopped off at the Crossbow stall, surrounded by fans and hangers-on. He handed me a pound coin.

'Go on, then,' he said, playing up to the crowd. I loaded the crossbow for him; he lifted it and aimed at the target, then shifted a few degrees to the right and shot the bolt into one of the prize teddies.

'Whoops!' he said. 'Straight through the heart!'

I was the only one not laughing. I was worrying about how I'd explain the mangled teddy to my brother.

My favourite job on North Pier was the Wiggle Wire. This was a revolving spiral of wire with an electric current running through it: you had to guide a metal hoop down the spiral from top to bottom without touching; the slightest contact completed a circuit and triggered the alarm, but if you touched the hoop on the metal base-plate you'd complete a different circuit and set a red light flashing, which meant you'd won a giant soft toy like a polar bear or Sesame Street Big Bird. Part of the job was mastering the technique so you could show people it was possible. It was all in the wrists; you had to keep your arms still and let the wire twist through the hoop; all you had to do was keep the plane of the hoop perpendicular to the wire and let things take their course – you had to efface yourself from the task and let the wire spiral up through the hoop at its own pace; if you tried to force it, you were lost. Once mastered, it was easy, and I'd make it *look* easy to hook the punters. Most of them were men, and soon they'd be four or five quid down but would push on regardless, goaded by wives or girlfriends, pride at stake now, and a low masculine competitiveness in the air, as if my demonstration had thrown a gauntlet, the Wiggle Wire a rite of courtship in which I figured as the rival mate that had to be seen off, outshone.

On North Pier we had a mobile unit of slot games, two ranks with a narrow aisle between them, and a hatch at one end for giving out change. We took turns squeezing into the shoulder-width space to sort and stack small-denomination coins into one-pound towers. You had to lock yourself in, and though this was the easiest job, with hardly any effort involved, the August heat was intense in there; the only fresh air came through a half-moon opening in the reinforced glass; you soon got cramp in your legs; you had to put up with the whirr of coin-operated cranes clutching at novelties and the non-stop electronic chirruping of the machines. It was when I was on change duty in the slot-game hutch that Clare bared her midriff to me, swinging her hips from side to side. She'd joined us late in the season; she was eighteen, sleek and tanned (she'd rented a sunbed for the summer, going halves with her sister), and very attractive, boys running at her heels. I think she flirted with me not because she found me desirable but because flirting came to her as naturally as breathing. One afternoon, when I was sitting at the change hatch, she left the Milk Can and wandered over, looking at me intently. The pier wasn't busy. She kept looking at me; she started to dance slowly in front of me; she pulled her red 'First Prize Games' polo shirt out from her jeans and lifted it to show her belly-button, her smooth tanned stomach. I didn't say anything; I just watched her dancing. Then I noticed a family loitering by the Milk Can: Clare put her hand over her mouth in mock guilt and ran back to take their money. It was early September, the season winding down. She waited for me to finish my shift at the Crossbow stall. She was flirting, but I was timid, anxious, self-interrogating; I couldn't let go of myself, however much I wanted to. Clare suggested we ride the Carousel. We were the only two people on it, and this was the last ride of the day, our gondola swinging through the half-light, red and yellow lights lurching round us, sliding and breaking on the glass panes of the Sun Lounge, salt breeze on our faces, views of the sea coming and going. I thought about putting my arm round her shoulders, but I didn't dare it. We left the Carousel and walked back up North Pier onto firm ground, and then we walked to the bus station, a desolate, deserted basement zone of grey concrete planes and dankness: she had to catch the last bus to Poulton. We sat on the kerb. She fished a packet of Silk Cut from her bag, opened it and pulled out a joint she'd rolled that morning. We passed it back and forth; I smoked it clumsily, hoping she wouldn't notice. My mouth went dry. We sat on the kerb until her bus came.

Some nights towards eleven o'clock I'd go with Martin to shut up the stalls and empty the money boxes at the end of North Pier. We'd have the place to ourselves, the machines dark and silent, and there was a sense of escape, as if we'd left the town behind us, the open boardwalk like the deck of a boat with wind sheeting across it and the long white fringes of high-tide waves riding their own phosphorescence to the sea wall. Look up and you'd see powerful searchlight beams sliding over the clouds, feeling out their tucks and contours; even on clear nights you didn't see stars – the town's myriad electric illuminations made a dome of light too dense for stars to shine through, and you navigated instead by the gaudy earthbound zodiac of the Pleasure Beach, the Big Wheel and the Golden Mile.

I was on the Milk Can on Central Pier when my exam results came through. I took a lunch break and asked the attendant to let me on the Big Wheel. There were overcast days when the grey of sea and sky merged without perceptible horizon seam: just the finger-slenderness of the three piers venturing out and the orange glow – like an ember, or somebody holding a match on the far side of the room – of a drilling rig's burn-off flare somewhere near the Isle of Man. I loved the way the Wheel lifted you slowly from the seethe and clamour of the pier. Soon you were eye-level with the gulls: looking back over your shoulder you'd see Blackpool spread out below like a model of itself; you could see the rollercoasters plunging and banking at the Pleasure Beach, the trams shrunk to toy dimensions on the esplanade. Sometimes the attendant yanked the brake lever and stopped the Wheel, leaving one bench dangling at the zenith; otherwise nothing marked the moment you were no longer going up but going down. I remember 'Maggie May' coming on, and the way the Wheel drew me down into the music and lifted me out again; I remember the attendant stopping the Wheel just as I could go no higher, and the way the mandolin's repeated figure grew louder and louder as if the music were coming up to meet me as I sank back down among the stalls. I sat on the Wheel for a long time, looking out to sea.

Thursday Esther Freud

It was five minutes before the end of the school day and I needed a wee. I could ask my teacher. He wouldn't mind. He might hesitate, might glance up at the clock, but he'd say yes, there was no doubt that he'd say yes. I'd had the same teacher since I was six – Mr Clark – and I was twelve now, old enough to wait five minutes for the bell. And I could wait. Of course I'd wait. I jiggled a little, shifted on my seat. Maybe I *should* ask, but the fact was, I didn't want to. Didn't want to ask for anything. Wished, suddenly, I never had to ask for anything again. So I waited, wriggling, a hot shiver running up my spine. Mr Clark was explaining homework. There was someone who didn't understand. Someone who wanted an extension: 'Couldn't we hand it in on Monday?' Mr Clark considered this. Come on, I hissed. And then the bell rang and I started to pack away my work, place it into my wooden desk. My insides were hot now, stinging, piercing my sides. I pressed my thighs together, but someone else had their hand up and Mr Clark was asking what was wrong. I tried to listen, but my brain was in too much of a hurry to hear. Come on, come on. I had one leg crossed over the other, my foot tapping fiercely up and down. And then finally, finally, everyone was standing, tucking their chairs into their desks.

Mr Clark waited, he wanted silence. The clock showed three thirty-three. He'd wait for ever, for the last squeak and whisper to subside. Come on! I was burning hot now. Could hardly stand. There was sweat breaking out on my forehead, collecting in the grooves behind my knees. Eventually he smiled and looked around. Goodbye, Class Seven, he said, and with a rumble we replied: Goodbye, Mr . . . But on the exhale of breath, on the soft sound of the Mister my bladder broke and a great storm of piss came rushing out. I stood and watched it, streaming out from underneath my skirt. I felt frozen, cut off from the world, and in that moment there was only one thing that was clear to me. This was the worst thing that had ever happened in my life.

And then it was over, and the noise of my class was all around me. Shouts and scraping as everyone pulled out their chairs, turning them upside down, clattering them on top of their desks so the cleaners could sweep. And just as if nothing had happened, people began to move towards the door. The girl to my right, her head bent, her mouth full of chewed-up hair, shuffled away shyly as she always did. I took courage and glanced to my left and, then, remembering, saw that the boy who usually sat there was away. I looked round. Maybe, maybe I'd been spared, but then from behind me came the cruel sound of a laugh. It was Bobby Wilcox. And he'd seen. Of course he'd seen. I spun around and caught him. Caught him looking, incredulous, his eyes wide open, his mouth hilarious with surprise. For a moment we both looked at it, the pool of pee, steaming slightly, and then just as his mouth opened to speak, I turned my eyes on him, and with the spit of a snake I warned him, 'Don't ever say a word about this, do you understand?' I must have been fierce because his head jolted back, and without looking at him again, I hurried from the room. I walked as fast as I could, pushing through the milling children, grabbed my coat, thank God that it was autumn, and without waiting for my usual crowd, for my sister, or my stepsisters, I walked as fast as I could down to the bus stop. I got there so quickly I caught the early bus and arrived home a whole half-hour before the others.

Thursday

I changed, hid my wet tights and skirt at the bottom of the laundry basket, and went and found my mother. My mother didn't know. She existed in that other time, when it still hadn't happened. 'Hello,' I said, pretending to be happy and I checked the clock and saw I still had twenty-five minutes before I'd be found out. Before she'd hear the news of my disgrace. Even now it would be out there in the playground, passing from mouth to mouth, forcing my sisters, for their own sakes, to jeer and jibe as well. But they weren't home yet and I still had time to pretend it wasn't true.

Eventually they came in. I scanned their faces, saw no signs there, nothing. If they knew, they weren't telling, and it was just possible they didn't know. Relief spread through me. I was safe. But only until my stepfather came home. He'd arrive straight from the staffroom where, among the steam of the kettle and the smoke from teachers' cigarettes, would be the news. 'Did you hear . . . ?' It would be shrouded in concern, but behind the hushed voices and kind eyes, there would be disgust. My stepfather might feel it was his duty to address the issue. Discuss it with me. Tonight. At supper. Or maybe he'd get me alone and ask me what was wrong. Why I was acting like a baby. Making a mess. Losing control of myself. He'd want to know, on behalf of my teacher, my class, the cleaner, if I was planning to do it again. Please God, that he doesn't say anything in front of the others. In front of me. I set my face against this conversation. I looked into the mirror, my mouth miserable, and set my eyes to 'No'. My mouth, the line of my hair: 'No'. I sat through supper without catching anybody's eye. Don't, I told them. Don't come near. Don't ask if I'm all right. I cleared the table. Helped with the washing-up. I did my homework, practised my cello until I was asked to stop. And then there was nothing left between me and my mother's goodnight kiss, the time, reserved for me, when she'd bend over my bed, talk to me, look me over, check to see how I was. Quickly I changed into my nightie. And then in a moment of inspiration I ran out and found her, gave her a quick hug and said I was going to bed now. I was tired. Goodnight.

I dived under the covers. Safe. It was a miracle. I'd escaped and then it hit me. It was Thursday and in a few hours' time it would be Friday. There was no avoiding it. I began to shiver in my bed. I could see it all unfolding, my class waiting for me, maybe in a circle round my puddle of cold wee. I lay awake. I'd make the night last as long as I could. Make myself too ill to go to school. But the next day came, hard as I tried to delay it, and I woke with no blocked nose, no fever, no energy left for lies, and so, with 'No' and 'Don't' branded hard across both eyes, I walked in to my class. I was the last one in, on the tail end of the bell, having spent ten minutes in the toilets, forcing out one drop of wee.

Without catching anybody's eye, I slunk down into my seat, accepting with relief that the puddle was gone. I worked hard, kept my head and my hand down. And at break I took the arm of my best friend, Esme, and led her out into the playground, away from the gangs and the groups of boys. Away from Bobby Wilcox and his smirk. Esme allowed herself to be led, accepted that from now on we should play, just the two of us, in a cave of rhododendron bushes that made an island between two lanes. We played, chatted, sank deeper than was usual into our imaginary world, and if she did know, I wove a spell around her so powerful that she soon accepted it was wiser to forget.

I waited all weekend, and all weekend nothing was said. On Sunday night I looked around the table. There were my three stepsisters, each with their own woes, my real sister, concerned with some feud of her own. There was my mother, sleepy with the demands of a toddler, and my stepfather, distracted by the pile

of unmarked essays, the trip to the buy-in-bulk warehouse where he'd forgotten to get flour. It seemed as
if I might be safe. I slept well that night for the first
time, and on Monday, the faces of my class looked less
threatening, swept clean with the amnesia of the
weekend. But on Wednesday I understood something
I hadn't realized before. There was no avoiding it,
Thursday would come around again. Thursday. What
if it happened, just the same? And a fear rose up in me
so bitter I could taste it in my mouth. I walked
through that Thursday in a sweat of dread. As soon as
I woke, I decided I would do everything in my power
to make it different. I found the clothes I'd worn the
week before and buried them in the back of my cupboard; even the pants, washed and folded in my
drawer, I shoved into the bin. Porridge, I'd eaten porridge last Thursday, so today, although I didn't like it,
I'd have egg. But hard as I worked, everything was a
hurdle. Should I eat my apple? There was nothing
else and I was hungry, but I'd eaten an apple last
Thursday at break, and look what had happened
then. It was true, I'd survived it, but I knew I wouldn't
survive it again.

Thursday followed Thursday. Each one as frightening as the last. It was waiting to get me. Trip me up.
And each week at three thirty, when the bell rang and

I'd been spared, I felt sick with relief. I began to pray to God. The God of Thursday. I bargained with him to spare me. I'd do my homework the day it was set, help at home, wash and sweep, sing to the baby, go to bed as soon as I was asked. And so in this way I struggled through a whole half term.

The Christmas holidays came, distracting me, soothing me with their timelessness, but the next term, starting cruelly on a Thursday, threw me back in to the grip of fear. It was overwhelming me, all this bartering and bargaining. It was taking up my energy, sapping the pleasure from my life. And then one day, in early spring, my stepfather asked if I'd be interested in going to Germany on an exchange. There was a notice in the staffroom, a family from Stuttgart were looking for a girl my age to exchange with their daughter for a term. 'Yes,' I said, before I'd thought it through. 'I'll go.' No one would know me there. There would be no Bobby Wilcox to give me secret looks, no Mr Clark with his kind smile; even Thursdays (and I knew this was crazy), Thursdays wouldn't know. It was April, I was almost thirteen, and with a light heart, and a bag packed with the two longest books I could find in the house, I set off to live with another family for three months.

In Germany there was plenty to distract me. There

was loneliness, and the realization that I couldn't understand one syllable of the south German dialect my new family spoke. There were long boring afternoons when school finished at one, and I had to accept that out of all seven Schulze children there was not one I could befriend. There was nothing to eat except pureed spinach, and potatoes, and then there was the embarrassment of not having anything to wear when my clothes became too tight. But I stayed there, never considering I could change my mind, and life slowly got better. Summer came and we went every afternoon to an enormous lake to swim. I made friends with a girl in my class, a teacher's daughter, who had a radio in her room and knew the words to English songs, and by the end of three months, almost without realizing it, I had become fluent in German, in the local dialect too, and the people I was staying with, my adoptive family, were kind and took me shopping and bought me three pairs of corduroy trousers in a bigger size that smelt of packaging and cardboard even after they were washed.

And then one day, only a few weeks before the end of my stay, I met a boy who was also on an exchange. His name was Adrian. His family came from Scotland but they were moving south, and in September he was due to start at a new school, which happened to be mine. Adrian was a year older than me, would be in the class above, and I said I'd look out for him next term. 'See you then,' he said. And my new German friend nudged me and giggled and said he was gorgeous, which, I agreed, he was.

At first I didn't see him. I looked out for him in the playground, craned to find him in assembly although inevitably he was two rows back, but then, one Thursday as our class waited to go into the science lab, waited for the group inside to come filing out, I saw him, and he smiled. I smiled back and from then on, I could hardly wait for Thursday – Thursday was the day I knew I'd see Adrian, could gauge from one week to the next how his feelings for me had grown. Thursday, miraculously, had become my favourite day, building in passion and feverish excitement until the following spring when we were thrown together at a party, my first experience of a darkened room with crisps and dip and music, and – the culmination of six months of longing – we kissed. I was almost fourteen. I had my first boyfriend, and even though he was kind and handsome and could take apart and reassemble a moped in the course of a weekend, the best thing about him was that he was new, and couldn't know.

And then, quite suddenly, during that spring term, my stepfamily split up. I was shocked, disorientated and upset, but I'd be lying if I didn't admit to some feelings of relief. Never again would I have to worry that my stepfather might take me to one side and grill me over the sordid events of that Thursday. For a year and a half, I'd waited and now, he'd missed his chance, it was too late. My sister left home, we moved to a new house and for the first time since that November afternoon I started to feel free.

I'm not sure if it was this new burst of liberation that gave me the idea, but when, the following September, a new girl joined our class, a girl called Dee Dee from as far away as America, I callously dropped Esme, my friend, so loyal since the age of six, and took up with Dee Dee. We sat together on the windowsills at lunch, our legs draped over the radiators and talked about boys and cigarettes and sex. We talked about New York versus London, about our mothers' boyfriends, about Adrian (now, in that fourteen-year-old way, a figure from the distant past), and I knew that whichever way our conversation swerved, the humiliation of that Thursday would never mistakenly slip out. Sometimes I'd catch sight of Esme, eating her lunch at a desk below, alone, making do at playtime with a gang of girls we'd previously scorned, but something in my heart had hardened, and I stuck with Dee Dee, never explaining, never attempting to talk to

Esme again, until I left the school at sixteen, and started in London on an entirely new life.

For ten years I never once thought of *Thursday*. I managed to forget the whole episode, never linked it in to anything else, until one night, late, I received a phone call. 'Hello?' The voice sounded tentative, unsure. 'This is Esme, you remember, from school?'

'Yes, yes of course.' The phone was in the bathroom. I must have pulled it in there earlier so as not to miss calls when I was in the bath, and now clutching the receiver, I sank down to the floor. 'How are you?'

'I never understood,' she started straight in, 'what happened. Why you went off with Dee Dee? Why you dumped me like that?' I could hear her shallow breathing, could hear the wrench in her voice as she struggled not to cry.

'I'm so sorry.' I had a sudden flashback of her baffled face, her lonely figure in the playground. 'I really am . . .' Guilt thumped in my chest. 'It was horrible of me.'

There was silence for a moment, and I thought, I'll do it. I'll tell her. But even after all those years I couldn't find the words. I couldn't tell her, just in case she actually didn't know.

'But you,' I said lamely, 'you went off with Tina in the end.'

'No.' She wasn't accepting it. 'It wasn't the same. And anyway she got expelled at Christmas for bringing in ouzo and drinking it on the swings.'

'Oh, yeah.' I laughed. How could I have not remembered? 'And um . . . Hilary and Zia, didn't you use to hang out with them?' I winced even as I said it. Hilary and Zia – the class swots. I could almost hear her shake her head in disbelief. 'But hey . . .' I said more lightly, wanting badly now to draw her in, 'isn't it nice to be grown up? To discover things don't matter quite so much?'

'Yes,' she said, slowly, unconvincingly. 'Yes,' and without leaving me her number, she hung up.

My Father's Girlfriends
Zoe Heller

My parents separated when I was four, or possibly five.
They had a long, untidy break-up, eked out over various adulteries and reconciliations, so it's hard to put a
specific date to it. At any rate, none of the women who
feature in my childhood memories of my father is my
mother. When my siblings and I saw him for birthday
dinners, or movie-outings, or trips abroad, the women
who came along were girlfriends: fragrant, international companions who talked to my father not in the
genial, domestic language of marriage, but in a strange,
coded banter. Some handled my father with a joking
sort of disdain. Others wheedled at him in baby voices.
Some were as silent and watchful as cats. Others threw
tantrums in public places. But like Bond girls, their
surface heterogeneity never obscured their identity as
a group. Even as a young girl, I could see that the girlfriends were a sorority of sorts. They embodied the

slightly louche glamour for which my father had traded in drear English domesticity.

My father was a Hollywood screenwriter. (His movies – *What Ever Happened to Baby Jane?*, *The Dirty Dozen*, *The Flight of the Phoenix*, *The Killing of Sister George* – bear the imprint of his rather bleak wit.) He maintained a base in London – a small, white-carpeted bachelor pad in St John's Wood that always smelled of roast beef and cigars – but he chose, for tax purposes, to spend the greater part of any given year in Los Angeles or Mexico. Or Italy. Or Spain. Every week or so, throughout my childhood, he rang home. I came to rather dread these phone calls. The idea was to exchange news, but it was never clear what, in my schoolgirl's life, really warranted recounting on an expensive foreign line. (Surely a person domiciled on the West Coast did not need to know about my upcoming bicycle proficiency test?) Those were the days in which all long-distance calls echoed. When my brother and sisters and I shouted into the receiver, our slightly stagy exhilaration would come trilling right back at us: 'HI, DAD! hi, Dad! HOW ARE YOU? how are you?'

Sometimes, during our school holidays, my father would send for us to join him abroad. It was on such a trip – a fortnight's sojourn in Mexico City – that we had our first encounter with one of his girlfriends.

Her name was Christa and officially, she had been employed to look after us. (My mother was usually in charge of arranging child care, but Shanny, the gawky Australian woman whom she had sent out with us on a previous holiday, had so displeased my father that this time, he had insisted on making the selection himself.) Christa lived in Germany and on the Saturday morning before we were due to leave for Mexico, my mother and I went to pick her up at Gatwick Airport. It took a long time for us to find her in the arrivals hall, but when at last we saw her teetering towards our sign, I recall my mother letting out an involuntary bark of hostile amusement. Christa was a very tall, slim Equadorian – a former Miss Equador as it turned out. She had hair the colour of tomato ketchup and wonderful, luminous skin, large areas of which she typically kept exposed. For her arrival in rain-sodden England, she had chosen to wear a diaphanous peasant blouse and four-inch platform heels, hand-customized with silver spray paint and stick-on stars.

The conversation in the car back to London was tricky. My mother asked polite questions in a remote, Lady Bracknell tone and Christa, who spoke only pidgin English, responded with a great deal of giggling. As we were getting out of the car in Primrose Hill, our milkman happened to be coming down the street in his electric float. The sight of Christa unfolding herself from the passenger seat so disoriented him that he crashed into a lamp-post. 'Oh Jesus,' Christa remarked in the untroubled way of a person used to causing traffic accidents. When the milkman emerged, staggering, from the smoking wreckage, he was grinning dreamily. I was eight years old and familiar with the cliche of women slaying men with the force of their sexuality. But this was the first time I had seen it enacted with such clarity.

In Mexico, Christa proved to be a thrillingly unsuitable chaperone. She took us out on shop-lifting expeditions to department stores. She gave my sisters and I makeovers using the vast supply of cosmetics that she carried with her in a handyman's tool box. She sunbathed by the hotel pool in obscene bikinis that she had fashioned herself out of tiny, crocheted triangles and curtain rings stolen from the hotel room. She incited a near riot when she strolled through Cheputapec Park in her Daisy Dukes and – what was then an unimaginably exotic jewellery item – a belly chain.

One night in our hotel suite, Christa told a story about asking my father what I, his youngest child, might like for my forthcoming birthday. 'More than anything else, Zoe wants her father's happiness,' she reported him saying. 'So the best birthday present you

could give her would be to have sex with me, tonight.'
There was much ribald laughter at this anecdote and
when I looked at my father, even he was snickering in
a vaguely shamefaced way. His wish, it seemed, had not
gone ungranted.

I don't recall being particularly bothered by this
incident. I was mildly indignant perhaps, at having
been cheated out of a birthday present. (If only Christa
had asked me, I could have told her that a box of
Caran D'Ache pencils would have been most acceptable.) But the unsolicited glimpse into my father's
wooing technique did not phase me. His nonconform-
ity to standard fatherly modes had long since been
established. He was not a stern paterfamilias. He said
'motherfucker'; he stubbed his Gauloises out in his
fried eggs; he had bullet holes in his stereo speakers
from the time he had misfired one of his handguns; he
had never asked me to perform a single household
chore. And he was not a cuddly, cosy Daddy, either. (If
ever I or one of my siblings attempted to embrace him,
he clapped us discouragingly on the back before swiftly
disengaging.) The idea of him wheedling for sexual
favours from the woman he had employed as our au
pair was interesting, certainly, but not so very shocking.

My father's relationship with Christa did not last for
long. She joined us again the following year in Ibiza,

but this time, her fiancé, a German dentist called Dieter, turned up halfway through the holiday. (On the morning of Dieter's arrival, Christa and my father pushed their beds apart and Christa moved her suitcases into my sister's room.) After that, we never saw her again.

In spite, or perhaps because, of the brevity of her appearance in our lives, I always regarded Christa as the Ur-girlfriend – the hallowed archetype of my father's taste in women. Various facets of her style – the cartoonish, girl-can't-help-it body, the outrageous wardrobe, the bad behaviour – did indeed turn out to be crucial motifs in my father's subsequent romantic history. My father was not an extroverted personality. He had a sly, ironic temperament. He liked to skulk in the corner of a room, subverting whatever was going on in its centre with dry, ruthless jokes. But in his choice of companions he betrayed a buried exhibitionist impulse. The girlfriends were status symbols, of course – guaranteed to inspire the slack-jawed envy of his male friends – but they were also portable entertainment: proxies for his desire to provoke and enrage.

Valeska, in particular, had a fearsome appetite for public confrontation. She came from Munich. The first time my father introduced us to her, we went out to an Indian restaurant in Hampstead, where she spent the evening making pellets out of the paper tablecloth and throwing them at other diners. Later, on the way home, she ran along the street, snapping off car antennae and arranging them in a bouquet for my father. I had never seen an adult behave in such a gratuitously unreasonable way before. It was intoxicating.

Physically, Valeska was a combination of bunny girl and running back: six foot tall, hipless, with huge shoulders and a vast, rigid bosom. (One of her previous lovers had been a plastic surgeon and he had given generously of his services.) Her hair was straight and orange, or yellow and curly, as a rule, but every now and then she would ring the changes with a wig – her favourite being a shoulder-length platinum bob which she wore when she wanted to look 'classy'. Her one unchanging tonsurial rule was No Bangs. 'A woman cannot be beautiful unless she shows her forehead,' she used to say. Her clothes tended to the sort of haute Germanic decadence found in mid-career Helmut Newton photographs: a lot of thigh-high leather boots, a lot of corsets, a lot of fur. But, rather endearingly, she had retained some pockets of preppy taste from her bourgeois upbringing. She liked hacking jackets, for example, and beige cashmere polo necks. (Beige, she once told me, was the 'wealthiest' colour.) The clash of the two aesthetics resulted in a fascinating, 'Teutonic sex worker visits the English countryside' look that was entirely her own.

She bestrode the world like a dotty colossus, dancing on tables, singing in the street, shouting at shop owners and taunting men in bars. This last activity often resulted in violence. On at least two occasions during the years I knew her, the injuries she sustained in bar brawls required plaster casts. Once, in a Munich club, a man broke her arm after she had torn his shirt apart in order to demonstrate the trick of 'making buttons dance'. Another time at a dinner party, she so provoked one of my father's friends by repeatedly calling him 'an ugly old potado', that the normally mild-mannered man rose up and socked her in the nose.

In retrospect, it is clear that Valeska had a drink problem, although I don't believe anyone gave it that name at the time. Her tipple of choice was Grand Marnier, which she drank in great thirsty draughts, like a medieval king knocking back his mead. The early stages of her drunkenness were often charming. She would tell amusing anecdotes about her ex-husband, the German army colonel, and sing British wartime songs that my father had taught her.

*

Monday night his hand was on my ankle
Choosday night his hand was on my knee
Wednesday night with great success he lifted up
  my blooming dress
In cholly, cholly cholly cholly cholly cholly Eng-land.

Inevitably, however, an uglier, more combative phase would ensue. Valeska didn't have politics as such, but her instincts were essentially fascist and she wasn't beyond castigating people as 'smelly little Jews' when she was in her cups. My father, who had come to England as a refugee from Nazi Germany, might have been expected to object to this. But he didn't. It somehow suited his perverse sense of humour to be romantically involved with an angry Bavarian anti-Semite.

Even though Valeska was around for at least four years, she never moved in with my father and they never owned anything jointly. They travelled together; they stayed for months at a time in each other's apartments, but the union did not progress any further. It was the same with all my father's girlfriends. Even when they were spending seven nights a week in St John's Wood, they never gave up the leases on their own places.

The open-ended nature of these arrangements

suited us children, I think. It is one thing, after all, to have Gilda in your life as an exotic auntie-figure; quite another to have her as your stepmother. Had the girlfriends ever set up house with my father, we would have had to adapt to their regimes, their world views, their home furnishings. No doubt we would have ended up rowing with them as bitterly as we did with our mother's second husband.

As it was, we could be unreservedly grateful for the girlfriends' entertaining strangeness, without any fear of having to live by their rules. They were scandalous fairy godmothers. They kept at bay the squally gloom that descends on purely familial gatherings. They dispensed beauty tips and gave us drags on their cigarettes. They confided tantalizing information about their rackety romantic lives. One girlfriend, Nikki, had had an affair with the footballer, George Best – a feat which, back in the seventies, made our mouths form fat 'O's of stupefaction. Another girlfriend, Sally, had a long-standing 'thing' with a married movie star. (Evidently, this relationship survived her brief liaison with my father because, more than a decade later, when I was in my twenties and working as a journalist, she and the movie star asked to borrow my London flat for one of their afternoon assignations.)

Rose, a blonde English woman who stayed with my

father for three years, used to invite me for sleep-overs at the St John's Wood apartment when he was away. After I'd scrubbed her back in the bath, we would lie together on my father's sinister black leather waterbed, and she would tell me the story of how my father had won her. (She had thought him 'an old fart', she said, and had only agreed to a second date after strenuous and protracted courting on his part.) Part of the reason that she and I loved this narrative so much, I think, was that it featured my father in the unlikely role of emotional supplicant. As a rule, my father played precisely the opposite part in both of our lives. It was we who wanted him to notice us – to talk to us, to tell us what he was thinking – he who kept us dangling.

The shared desire to conquer my father's remoteness – to scale his battlements – was something of a theme in our relationships with all the girlfriends. We never really competed with them – my father had obviated the need for such contests by being equally inaccessible to all of us – but there was often a subtext of friendly commiseration in our conversations about him. I remember staying at my father's one night when I had had a row with my mother. I was feeling desperate in the way that you do when you are a discontented teenager and your life is still hopelessly circumscribed by adults. I couldn't bear the idea of returning to my mother's house, but I could see that I wasn't going to be able to sleep on my father's sofa for much longer. I wanted him to say, 'You never have to go home again. Come live with me and be my little helpmeet.' But he was not going to say that. He wanted me out. It was late at night and I was sitting up doing my economics homework when Amanda, the girlfriend he was seeing at the time, came out of his bedroom. She was in an agitated state. 'Your father is so cold,' she whispered angrily. 'He never shows me physical affection unless it's for sex.' Later, I would laughingly report this incident to my friends, as an excruciating case of Too Much Information. But it wasn't really. It was soothing to hear her rage; to luxuriate for a moment in the camaraderie of the rejected.

Towards the end of his life, my father did a very unlikely thing. He began an affair with a communist member of the Italian parliament. Luciana was no less glamorous than any of the previous girlfriends. (European communists do not subscribe to the asceticism of their Anglo-Saxon counterparts.) In fact, her beauty was so famous in Italy that when the ageing Italian president Pertini was once asked by a reporter if he had any regrets in life, he is said to have replied with croaky wistfulness, that he was only sorry 'not to have slept with Luciana Castellina'. Nevertheless, Luciana did represent a dramatic departure from my father's standard type. She was close to my father in age. (They were both in their fifties when the relationship began.) She held passionate political convictions. She had a busy, high-profile career. None of the other girlfriends had ever had proper jobs to speak of. They might have dabbled in antiques, or modelled a bit, or freelanced in the movie industry, but their real employment had always been girlfriendhood. Sometimes, when my father travelled in Europe with Luciana, he would be greeted as Signor Castellina.

My father was proud of Luciana's achievements – proud and slightly intimidated. He called her 'Madame Mao'. When her friends on the English left came to visit, he liked to tease her by lurking in the kitchen, with a tea towel wrapped around his head, imitating the ever-so-humble stance of a devoted spouse. 'Oh, me, I'm just Jenny Marx,' he'd say, refusing her pleas to come and join the earnest discussion in the living room. It was an odd pairing. Neither wanted to settle permanently in the other one's country, so they took it in turns to stay with each other. Had my father lived, it is unclear how they would have resolved this geographical dilemma. Perhaps they would have carried on commuting into old age. As it turned out, my father suffered an aneurysm while playing tennis one day, and died at the age of fifty-nine.

My mother and Luciana attended the funeral, but none of the other girlfriends. We had already lost touch with most of them, by then. Rose, I know, ended up marrying a rich fishmonger. Valeska died shortly before my father did. She was found murdered in her Munich flat: run through with an antique sword that had formed part of her baroque interior-decoration scheme. The assailant was never apprehended. Christa, Nikki and all the others have vanished into the ether.

There is one girlfriend with whom I have remained in contact. She lives in Los Angeles and is the honorary godmother of my daughter, Francesca. It was she who closed the circle of the family romance several years ago, by introducing me to Francesca's father: an American of Russian-Jewish descent who is sixteen years my senior, somewhat saturnine in temperament and – with galling Freudian symmetry – a Hollywood screenwriter.

Danny in the Car
Nick Hornby

So it's a lovely, sunny, crisp London Sunday morning, and I'm in the car with my son Danny. Danny is six and autistic, and he loves the car; it really is a bubble to him, and nobody can burst it. When he's strapped into the back seat he's safe. No other kids can get in his face like they do out in the world, where people fly at him, unpredictably and ungovernably like asteroids towards a spacecraft; and nobody will make him eat food he doesn't want to eat, and the side window is a videotape that never needs changing. He likes to know where he's going, though, so he's memorized all the significant routes in his world. (This, incidentally, is one of the enduring mysteries of autism. Danny only occasionally remembers that the sequence beginning 'Ready' and 'Steady' is completed by the word 'Go'. So how has he managed to construct a mental street map of the entire London metropolitan area?) The route to school is OK, because he likes school; the

Danny in the Car

route to Grandma's house is OK too, not only because he likes Grandma, but because she lives fifty-odd miles from London, so he gets to stay in the car longer. The route that's not OK is the route to the park. The park's too close to home, which means that the journey's over before it's properly begun, and someone, a bad person, his dad, will make him get out of the car. But it's a lovely, sunny, crisp Sunday morning. We're going to the park.

He starts to yell at the top of Delancey Street in Camden, when we don't turn left into Albany Street. That left turn he sees as his last chance – school was ruled out ten minutes ago, when we didn't turn into Liverpool Road after crossing Holloway Road at Drayton Park. See, Albany Street takes you onto Euston Road, and Euston Road leads eventually to the motorway and Grandma's house. But from Delancey Street we go straight across into Regent's Park Road, on our way to Primrose Hill. Doesn't that sound nice, Primrose Hill? Not to Danny it doesn't. The yells get louder when we stop, and reach a sweat-inducing pitch when I open his door. 'Come on, Dan,' I say, in my best fun voice. 'We're going to the park. The swings. The see-saw.' He just turns the yellometer up to eleven. I try to lead him out by the hand, but he snatches it away and grabs hold of something, the seatbelt, anything that will anchor him inside, so I end up dragging him out by his ankles. A couple of people look at us as they walk past. They don't say anything, but one day, I'm sure, someone's going to report me and I'll be arrested.

There's a certain irony to this. I learned to drive at the age of forty-one, entirely because of Danny. I didn't really want to learn, and I have a mild phobia about driving, but public transport, which had served me well all my adult London life, was becoming less and less fun. Danny loves going on trains and buses, of course, but sometimes he didn't want to get off when I wanted to get off, and sometimes he wanted to get off before our stop, and sometimes he decided that he didn't want to wear any trousers on the top deck of the number 19, and though I won all these battles of will because I'm bigger than him, I wasn't always in the mood to fight them in public, and in any case, I may not always be bigger than him, in which case we will be fighting properly. They can be pyrrhic victories anyway, these fights with autistic kids. Danny's best friend from school once kicked up such a fuss about having his hair cut at the hairdressers that he had to be held down by his mum and his nanny, at which point a woman ran over and started pummelling them both with her fists. Sometimes I silently

Danny in the Car

dare someone to say or do something, just so as I can tell them why I'm having to be so cruel, and hopefully make them feel terrible in the process. Danny's friend's mum made the pummelling woman feel terrible. She ended up bursting into tears. Sometimes, on a bad day with Danny, the thought of making a complete stranger burst into tears is extraordinarily attractive.

So, anyway. I took driving lessons for eighteen months, and slowly, slowly overcame my fear, and nothing, I felt, after every awful, juddering, fear-filled sixty minutes, could have demonstrated more dramatically how much I loved my son. I passed my test first time, and I bought a little four-door Peugeot that I thought he'd love, so I could drive him to places like the park. And is he grateful? Is he hell, the little sod. He's holding on to his seatbelt for dear life and screaming while I try to pull him backwards onto the pavement.

Eventually he can hold on no longer, and I lift him out and put him down, and after a brief pause during which he recovers his composure and stops yelling, he roars off towards the park gates. Because another thing Danny's forgotten until this very second is that he *loves* the park. He *loves* the swings and the see-saw, and spinning round and round on the grass until he's dizzy. And it's a lovely, sunny, crisp Sunday morning, and, hey, there's an empty swing, and literally within ten seconds he's full of smiles and happy anticipation, and there is no trace whatsoever in his face of the ankle-pulling trauma to which he was so recently and cruelly subjected. And I want to find the couple who may or may not have had a disapproving look on their faces when they saw me committing awful acts of violence, and show them just how joyful he is now, but of course they're not around. Which is maybe just as well, because in a while I'm going to have to find a way to get him out of this swing.

Daddy Julie Myerson

You enter this world on 13 March 1927, a bitter evening, I think, cold – cold and dark and wet. My Daddy, being born. Your birth is a long and drawn-out thing, said to be painful and hard and dirty. Not worth it, your mother later concludes. No, not even for a boy.

Geoffrey Denys Pike. Second child, only son, swirl-haired baby of the family, sepia-shawled and gazing out into the nowhere of the ruched velvet photographic studio. One day you'll be a real boy – the son your father half fears, half hopes for. Belted trousers and slipping-down socks, side-parted hair, peashooters and Brylcreem. A happy boy in a blazer and flannels. Then an RAF private, a drummer in a band in ENSA, a factory owner, a manufacturer, a vacuum former and hot-foil blocker.

Also: fiancé, husband, father, divorcee – later, grandfather and then, sometime after that, suicide.

Daddy

My Daddy. A suffocated heart in a small concrete garage. Deprived of oxygen, hope and love – whisky-fuelled exit on the edge of the year. Except you know none of this yet. In the shrill spring of 1927, your future waits, tightly wrapped and shiny and as full of possibility as the next baby's.

The minutes and then the hours tick by. Nursery hours, nursery silence – milk puddings, rabbits, muslin, woollen shifts. A bird – beak packed with fluff – alights on the windowsill, looks in briefly, flies away. You don't see him, but your hands curl and uncurl. A small posset of sick slips from the corner of your mouth. Mostly the nurse feeds you, but now and then you suck from a glass bottle held by a hand heavy with jewels. You are rapt. The bracelet clinks against the glass and you watch, barely breathing in case it goes away. But then your breath returns and the hand is gone. Sharp click of shoes going away. Your bottle is left propped against a dark wool cushion and you suck alone in an even darker place. Alone at five months with your milk and your shadowy hiccups.

Another photo shows you sprawled, helpless and drool-lipped, on a plaid rug next to your toothier sister. She looks pretty – curly-haired, smocked, eager to please. She looks . . . about five. You look alarmed. I wonder whether your mother puts these on display –

birth trophies, sombre reminders of the Never Again
– or whether they remain safe in the darkness of a
drawer or cupboard? Her cupboards are immaculate
and smell of Dubonnet. She is an uncluttered person,
your mother. She walks across lawns, small crocodile
bag dangling from one palm. She is with someone else
but she's looking straight ahead, at the camera. Later,
by the river, she bites into a white triangle of sandwich
and is caught, hand over mouth. Or sits on a bench on
a foreign terrace, sandalled feet propped on a wall,
gazing out for the photo. She makes you set a tripod
up on the grass and asks you to snap her. Chin up,
eyes wide. My Granny.

By the time I know her she is wrinkled, balding,
dentured, hefty-breasted – though she continues to
wear high heels, fur coats, stockings, jewellery, to the
end of her life. But once upon a time she was a tall,
slim, golfing person – a woman with a handbag and a
perm. A woman you might meet to socialize with.
Bridge or golf or cocktails. The managing director's
wife. My Granny. Staring out from a car window with
a slight frown on her face. Unsympathetic? Unsenti-
mental, she would say. She freely admits to preferring
birds and dogs to people. Dogs on her Christmas
cards, on her sideboards; birds on her notelets, her

tablemats. Tits and sparrows hanging from the monkey nuts outside her cold back-bedroom window.

You are born into money. Not so much, but enough. Industrial money, smoky, sweaty money. Enough for maids and cars and jewellery. Enough to be used against people. Your father's hosiery factory was set up by his father before him – Alfred Pike Limited of Nottingham. Hosiery Manufacturers. Vitaknit Underwear for Health. Tel. 760656. The Ayr Street Works – a frowny, dark brick street with derelict buildings, smashed and boarded-up windows, buddleia forcing through cracks in city walls. Stray dogs, old garbage, smells of ammonia and exhaust.

After school, when the fog and dusk comes down, we go there – to those huge draughty factory rooms, windows thick with a century of smoke and grime and clocking in and out. It gets darker. Windows fade to black and we keep our coats on because we aren't staying long. We're never staying long, because you have work to do. Our Daddy, smoking and standing and adding up figures. Costing. Invoicing. All for ladies' knickers, you say and you think it's funny, it makes you snigger and when you do that smoke comes out of your nose and I think of the connection between your mouth and your nose and I have to make my mind look away or else my tummy drags and falls like I'm going to be sick.

When I am two, I spill wine on a guest at Christmas. Uncle Dwight; except he's not my uncle. You carry me up the stairs to change me. I remember the smell of your shoulder, the safety of your grasp. I remember that I love you for ever then.

Knickers are bad but not as embarrassing as the girl at school called Joanna Smellie who (really, truly) lives on Nicker Hill. Anyway, the knickers aren't even normal knickers, they're bloomers, which is worse. Big huge knickers for fat ladies' bottoms, floppy knickers – so floppy you can't even think about it. But we do. We think about ladies' bottoms as we rush up and down the endless corridors and giggle at the other ladies who sit in rows working the machines, bobbins whirring, ciggies gathering ash in overflowing ashtrays.

We're allowed to pick up scraps of fabric from the floor to keep for dolls' clothes. As long as we don't get in the way, you say. So we train our eyes on this crucial bottom layer of the world. Our own three pairs of beige wool feet stomp and slide around in brown sandals, while the ladies' feet – bunioned and perspiring under the machines – wear tan stockings and tattered slippers. They come on the bus in zipped boots and change by the lockers. If we bend low enough we can see everything – veins and nylon slips and all. We like the look of all those feet pressing down on the pedals – sometimes they let us try but the pedals are stiff and we can't. You're quite fond of your ladies, though you don't know them all by name. They work like blacks, you say approvingly, and that makes me think of chimney sweeps – rows and rows of them, sooty-faced, pressing down on the stiff pedals.

Sometimes we smell the wool, smoke and paper smell and can't stop sneezing, and then the old man Mr Lichfield with his stained trousers and bald shiny head comes and says 'Bless you!' We think he's religious. He has his own office, with a green felt table with shiny balls on it. We like the pink one best, because we're girls. If we were boys it might be blue or red. 'Or black,' I remind my sisters. 'Boys like black.' In Nottingham there is a hotel called the Black Boy. A hotel for chimney sweeps, perhaps.

When you are a baby you have no idea you will one day be sent to work at the knicker factory, boss of the place, son of the old boss, king of them all. Maybe that's why you cry – because you can feel the future bearing down on you and you know it's ladies' underwear. Twinlock, jersey knit, singlets and pants. You cry even louder and your mother puts you in a room as far away as possible and shuts the door. She can't stand the sound of it, just as she can't stand lots of other things in the world. If she could, she might just shut the door on herself. Instead, she listens to the sound of you and picks at her nails. 'Can't someone shut that baby up?' You lie and cry, heaving and heaving, until the final heave sends you inexplicably off to sleep. A small bird alights on the windowsill, coaxed by the sudden silence. You don't see him, you are sunk in blackness, in sleep.

When I am five you take me to school and tell me we're late. Late for prayers. You leave me in the dark, potato-smelling vestibule where I wait so long I wet myself. I tell you this later, between great lurching sobs, and you laugh. You say it's funny. You say, don't worry, it won't happen again.

Two things that belong to you, to my Daddy. One, a heavy pewter cigarette lighter, I think it's from India, ribbed and shiny, that you can run your fingers over. It has green felt on the bottom so it doesn't scratch the polished furniture, a hot violet flame that stays straight and steady when you click the top down. And two, a big round ashtray where you press the button and it spins and tips the ash down inside. This is a nifty invention, you say. It keeps the ashtray spanking clean, look, and hides the smell. I nod a yes, but I know that it doesn't. I've seen the flat surface of the ashtray mottled with dead ash. And I know that when you press down and make it spin, you have to hold your breath or you taste old man, old trousers, old cigarette, on the roof of your mouth.

But you aren't a smoker when, at six or seven years old, they put irons on your legs. They say you have a weak heart, that you can't walk straight. Well, you can't now, that's for sure. You are a cripple – you are the shiny painted boy with the caliper and the dog, who stands outside paper shops with a slot in his head where the money goes in. And then, a year later, the irons come off and you are told that's it, you can go, you are fit now. Except your mother seems to like you even less. You were useless to her before, but now there's no excuse. (One night after the irons come off, you lie in your bed in the dark and something exactly the same size as you lies down on top and presses on your chest, you can't breathe and you think you're going to die. You shut your eyes and when you open them again it's gone. You say a few swear words under your breath, the only ones you know.)

But you won't be called a weakling. You decide to take up a hobby. You make model aeroplanes out of balsa wood. At first from a kit, and then from your own design. Propelling pencil, tracing paper, calculations. This is your precious thing – time alone with the taste and smell of glue in your ears, your eyes, your nose. You won't be called a weakling. You will be an aircraft designer. You are a boy of ten and a half with a hobby. One day you will do great things with it.

NOTTM MAN'S MODEL PLANE
BEATS WORLD RECORD

The plane was designed, built and flown at Tollerton Aerodrome by Mr Geoffrey Pike of Watcombe Circus, Nottingham. To beat the Russian record of 1 hr 2min 30 sec, set up by P. Velitchkovsky in 1952, the young Nottingham man spent hundreds of hours designing, testing, stripping down and rebuilding his plane before he was satisfied that he stood a chance . . . (from *Nottingham Guardian & Journal* circa 1955)

But that's all in the future. You are ten or eleven when you lean out of an upstairs window and take a shot at a boy in the street with your pea-shooter. You don't know the boy – you think he's called Kenneth, but he's just a walking target to you – and you can't stop laughing when he doubles up in pain. Pow! Aaaargh! But you're told it's not funny; you're told you've hurt him. You've done him so much harm, in fact, that his parents have to come round and give you a piece of their mind. They might even speak to the school.

'Why?' your mother snaps. 'What's it to do with the school?' She doesn't give in, your mother. A tiny bruise, she says, that's all it is. Nothing that a lump of ice won't cure. She doesn't offer tea or a drink or condolences. She keeps them standing in the cold porch. You are quite proud of that – of how frosty and unapologetic she is and you think that's it, it's over. But then when they've gone she asks your father to belt you, beat you, do whatever it takes. But Ernest is soft. He does it half-heartedly. His wrists don't work. You laugh at him so he does it a bit harder. You hit out at him and he yelps and shuts himself in his room with the sherry bottle. You are only ten and you've hit your father. You can feel your blood moving in your body, a hot, liquid army you can't control. It's not a good feeling.

I am seven when you start telling me ghost stories – stories of eyes and mouths in the dark. Stories from your childhood, stories from the war, from factories, from old people and young people and dark cities I know nothing of. None of it's serious. Fear is funny, you say. Personally, you don't believe the stories. You believe nothing – not ghosts or fairies or Jesus or Santa. All a load of balls, you say. I lie awake and have to turn the light back on. The balls are everywhere. I don't sleep. I stare at the acid yellow of the bulb till the birds start.

Poor Daddy. A year or so later, when your face and body are changing shape but your mind is still mostly on wood and glue and pins, you ask a girl round to tea, but you forget to tell your mother and when the little girl rings the door bell, she answers and gives her a chilly look, says she knows nothing about an invitation to tea and turns her away. 'Oh,' says the girl with some passion, 'but I have to come to tea now. I put clean knickers on!'

When you tell us this story, more than three decades later, you can't stop laughing. You're washing the car and you have to lay the hose across the bonnet and stop, you're laughing so much. Clean knickers. She put clean knickers on! Isn't that just so good? But, though we try to laugh, we're frantic to know what happened next. Did Granny give in? Did the little girl stay to tea after all? Your face doesn't change, you suck on your cigarette, shake your head. 'Oh no, your Granny turned her away. She wasn't having it. She didn't know anything about it, you see.' 'But – poor girl,' I say, thinking of how awful she must have felt all the way home. 'I daresay she got over it,' you reply.

The blood army moves in your body. Some mornings you wake and the bed sheets are scattered with wet. You don't know what's happened but you hate yourself. If you were an imaginary person you'd stop thinking about yourself right now – extinguish yourself for ever – make all of this disappear. But you're not, you're here and that's a thing you have no control over. Your body is stuck with your mind and vice versa. War's coming and all over Nottingham they're lining people up. Or that's what your Uncle Horace says. He's going to fight. You're too young to fight, you're only twelve – but even if you weren't twelve, even if you were older than that, you'd still get out of it because of your hammer toes. That's your father's reason too – it's a medical condition, a deformity that gets you out of war. Except that everyone knows the reason your father isn't fighting is because he's soft. He's a drunk, your friend Alan tells you, and you clout him hard for it, because you think he might be right.

If all the soldiers die, you think, who will be left? Just the mothers and the children and a whole lot of men with hammer toes? Your mother would be good at war. She is spectacularly ruthless. She turns away little girls and sacks maids by the handful. When she thinks you are taking too much sugar in your tea, she pours in a whole bagful and forces you to drink it till you are sick. She does not love you – none of her actions describe love in any way – but she wants you. Or, she does not want anyone else to have power over you. The idea of you marrying makes her feel physically sick. But you're not marrying. You're making aeroplanes.

Disaster overtook the plane on its ninth attempt to top the record on Easter Monday. For no accountable reason, the model, packed with high-precision radio equipment and delicate valves, spiralled into the ground, destroying the forward end of the fuselage. Aware that the next day, Easter Tuesday, would be the last chance he would have for some time, Mr Pike worked on the wreckage of his plane all night and rebuilt the nose and battery storage compartments. She was airworthy again!

Balsa Wood, Araldite, Engine Fuel, Aileron. These are words from my childhood – words I learn at the same time as Milk, Egg, Teddy Bear, Cat, Cup. You want to be an inventor. You leave school at fifteen, but you know more general knowledge than the average boy. Spellings, geography, the speed and weight of objects – these are the things that you always knew. You have no trouble with maths or science or the logic of things. It's not your fault you had to go into ladies' underwear. You could have been a great inventor, you always said – if only other people hadn't got there first.

When I am eleven I come in to get the *Radio Times* and see you hitting my mother. The TV is on. She is on the floor. You are a heavy shape, moving angrily where you shouldn't be. Two grown-ups too near to the floor. I close my eyes and leave the room. I hear sounds for a long time. I try not to think about what they might be.

When you are twenty-five you have your first girl-friend – a sweater model. You don't tell your mother. When I am five or six, I find a photo of her in your workshop.

'Who's this, Daddy?'

'An old girlfriend. She was a sweater model.'

'What's a sweater model?'

'Someone who models sweaters.'

I gaze at the photo. The woman is sitting on a car,

leaning back in a stupid way. She has yellow hair and dead eyes. She is wearing a sweater and her breasts look sharp and pointy in it, as if they'd hurt you if you bumped into her. I am astonished at the shape of those breasts, nothing like the vague, squishy softness I feel when my mother hugs me to her. Now, though, I know what's most astonishing. Not the sweater model's breasts but the fact that you didn't have a girl-friend till you were twenty-five. What happened? Were you so scared? Did your mother turn them all away?

You do National Service. You go into the RAF and then into ENSA, where you have a ball, you later say. Best time of your life, playing the drums in a band. Apart from aeroplanes, music is your single biggest passion. You can't read a note, never could, don't want to learn – but you have natural rhythm; you play by ear. You drum your way to the Far East, to Burma and Singapore, and see amazing things: sea snakes, phosphorescence, an egg frying on the wing of a plane. Then you come back home to Nottingham and, apart from a brief honeymoon in Nice, you never leave the country again.

'But, Daddy, why don't you ever go abroad?'

'Why would I? What's there that I'd want to see?'

Daddy

'But – so many things! So many different experiences.'

'I've seen all I want to see. What's the point of travelling when you can see it all on TV?'

This isn't really what you say. It's a guess. In fact, I can't imagine what your answer is, would be, would have been. I never asked you why, never thought to, never dared. When I was young, I was too young and untravelled to think to ask. When I was older, I was much too afraid. And then you were dead. You died in your car, but it was in the garage, going nowhere.

There is a picture of you in the Far East, fag in mouth, bare-chested, holding up a bunch of bananas. You look so happy – happy and pleased with yourself. Whole life in front of you, Daddy. What did you think it would be? Did you think you'd run away from your mother in the end, plan your escape, make it, be a drummer in a band?

When I am almost twelve my mother tells me she's going to leave you – that it will happen soon; that things will be better then; that I'm to tell no one; that she will make it OK; that life will be our friend. She apologizes for crying in front of me. She kisses me. She is strong.

You meet my mother when your car breaks down outside her father's office and you ask to use the phone to call for help. She is a brunette behind a type-writer, slim and sweet in her cotton dress, hastily stubbing out her cigarette when her father comes in. You take her out a couple of times and then you ask her to marry you. She says, yes, oh yes. It's 1959 and you are thirty-two and she is twenty and she is the perfect opposite of the sweater model. My mother has lit-up eyes and a look of expectation always – her face says it's about to be Christmas or a party. But you never give her parties. Almost from the start, she is lonely with you.

It's a shock. She never thought, when she said yes to you, that it would be like this – you in your work-shop building aeroplanes, she sitting alone and reading the *Nottingham Evening Post* or polishing floors, boiling milk, dusting skirting boards. She thought you might grow tired of your hobby, be with her, start a family.

Watched by observers and time-keepers, the model plane, which is powered by a two-ounce 87 cc motor and weighs 3 lb, took off very slowly after a 50-yard run on the ground and only just lifted itself into the air, for it was carrying 8 ounces of fuel.

Daddy

The plane circled Tollerton airfield. Then, after 50 minutes flying, with only 12½ more minutes left to beat the Russian record, the tiny engine started spluttering, cut out, and then, missing badly, fired again.

One autumn night, early in the marriage, she considers leaving and going home to her mother but, searching all her pockets for loose change, realizes she doesn't quite have the bus fare. You have no idea about any of this. You are at that very moment mixing Araldite with a matchstick, sliding a slick of milky white gum along the pale balsa rib of a plane called Jane. It's a precision moment. Too much glue and it will ooze out and spoil the clean line of the wood. Too little and it will come apart later. Jane – 'Plane Jane', a pun, you like that – is your own design. Like the servo mechanisms you designed. She's going to have black wings and a yellow undercarriage, Jane is.

'But, Mummy,' I say when she lies crying in my room and tells me about her plan to leave and how we'll be a different sort of family and all that, 'what about Daddy? What will he do? Won't he be upset? What about him?'

Do I say this? I've no idea, no memory. Or do I just

wait for her to do something, to change it all, to make life lighter for us?

While you work, you watch TV at the same time. *Double Your Money* is on. Now and then you look up, laugh under your breath. Later, your young wife brings you a cup of tea. You mutter a thank you, but you don't look up so you never know that she's been crying. That night in bed she tells you she'd like a baby. It would at least be company, she says, something to do in the evenings when you're in your workshop. All right, you say, because you can't really think of a reason to say no.

I am born on 2 June 1960, Julie Susan, black-haired, blue-eyed, a birthmark on my bottom. You are glad I am a girl. You like girls. You are relieved that my arrival barely seems to disturb your routine. On my first birthday, I wear a white lace dress and talk on a small plastic phone in the middle of a daisy lawn. On my fourth birthday, I get a doll called Janet-Mary with eyes that open and close. By then I have two sisters – their eyes open and close and they make a noise as well. For my fifth birthday, I get a doll that makes a noise when you tip her backwards. On my ninth birthday we've moved to the country and I eat American doughnuts sitting on a tractor seat. I get a sewing box with an upholstered lid. For my twelfth birthday, you pay for me to go up in a glider – high above the clouds, silence, perfection. For the first time, I understand about your hobby, the thing that still keeps you away from us – shuts you in your workshop, takes you to your flying field, even (once) on Christmas Day.

'There was only one thing to do: climb for height so that if the engine did cut out altogether we could still remain airborne for some time by gliding,' Mr Pike told a *Guardian Journal* reporter. He took the plane up to 2,000 feet and then, as the engine seemed to have recovered, spun her earthwards to 100 feet in eight seconds.

You do all the normal father things. You kiss us goodnight, tell us jokes, drive us to school and take us swimming at weekends. One Sunday we run over a pheasant on the way back from the swimming baths at Bingham. You stop the car and wrap the still warm body in a towel. 'Mummy will cook it,' you say, as we sob in grief and pity.

It is plucked and left to hang in the back kitchen, a bald and terrible greeting for us every day for a week after school. It is my last memory from the time of living with you – that bird hanging there, beak rimmed and sealed with blood, a casualty of the swimming run.

I am twelve when she leaves you. She leaves in the middle of the night with half the furniture, her three daughters, all the pets. There is a dog, a rabbit, an Aylesbury duck, a budgie and a hamster. We're all together, all in it together, she says. You get back to your home which is half empty and you call the police.

Why didn't I tell you? you want to know. You were twelve years old, Julie. You should have known. You should have called me as soon as you knew what she was doing. I take this as a betrayal. You don't love me. I blame you.

'But, Daddy. But how?'

'You should have called me. That's all I'm saying.'

'Yes, Daddy, but how?'

'Gone to a call box. You know how to use a call box, don't you?'

'Yes, but—'

'Instead, you did nothing. You let her get away with it. That's how much you love me. At least I know that now.'

Daddy

'But, Daddy – my Daddy!'

Eighteen years later and it's the edge of the year, freezing cold, stars in the night sky. You are sixty-four and you don't think you can go on much longer. You've been to Spar and bought a tin of beans, a bottle of Scotch, a bottle of Fairy Liquid. The receipt and the change are on the counter in the kitchen where you've washed-up your last pan, your last cup.

I am fourteen when you come and kiss me in my bed in the half-empty house, the same house where we always lived, but where we now visit you every other weekend, as the courts decided. Your footsteps on the stairs. I shiver. My bed is cold. There used to be normal things in this house – possessions, toys, rugs, furniture. When she left, our mother took half of everything and you didn't replace it. Why should you? you said. You said it was her punishment – that we should have to bear the consequences of her ruthless, selfish actions.

So the house is cold and bare, our beds freezing. Our voices echo on the landing. We get sore throats. Our mother buys us electric blankets to take with us when we visit, but we don't dare ask to plug them in. We know what you'll say. We know you won't want *her* blankets using *your* electricity. Why should she get her way? Why should we benefit? You light a cigarette.

Hate crackles around the house. But still you come up for your goodnight kiss.

I pull my nightie right down, over my feet. You put your whisky-wet lips against my ear and you blow. It's a joke, you say, it's not serious. I shiver and shiver. I can't bear your mouth near my head. I don't tell you. I feel sorry for you – sorry and disgusted and afraid all at once. The worst thing a girl can feel for her father.

You've wiped the draining board and left the dish-cloth wrung out on the side. You've drunk enough Scotch to make your walk a little unsteady but your end a little steadier.

I am sixteen. You tell my school you won't pay my school fees any longer. This long is enough. Never mind that I am a bright girl, who exactly do I think I am? You left school at fifteen and look at you. And, anyway, why should I benefit from having divorced parents? Why should a father shell out, just because a mother left?

When the court rules that you have to pay, you write me a short letter. Biro, Basildon Bond. You tell me you're not sure what you feel about me any more. You tell me you've taken the advice of a psychiatrist. You tell me it might be better if we don't see each other any more.

Daddy

My Daddy!

You think of a joke you heard on TV last night and you almost smile but the skin of your face won't stretch. You approach the thermostat carefully as if it is a fierce dog – put out your hand and turn the heating down. You don't like waste. You don't like life. You go slowly to your car.

To cheers and congratulatory shouts, the plane beat the Russian record and then flew for another 30 minutes and 19 seconds to set up a new world and British record of 1hr 32 min 49 sec.

The float chamber, servo mechanism and radio receiver in the plane were designed and built by Mr Pike, who has received an order for 2,000 servo units from an American firm.

It's almost midnight when you turn the key in the ignition, open all the windows, feel the warm vibrations. You keep this car so clean, vacuumed and beige and airless. You'd like a ciggie but you mustn't. In your head, birds are flying around and you smell the leaden fumes and try to breathe them in but you panic and turn off the ignition and open the door and lurch out of the garage. It's not that you can't do it, it's just . . . you need another drink. You'll have another drink and then it'll be easy. No point in rushing. You'll have another go in a minute.

I am twenty-eight. My first baby is a boy, your first grandson, first grandchild. The birth is joyous, painful, scary, wonderful. He's eight weeks old and I take him to see you – trembling because it's been more than ten years. He is all in white, hands curling and uncurling, hair a swirl of black just like your own. You are cool, civil. You pour me a drink. You glance at the baby. You decline to hold him. 'Maybe if it was a girl I would,' you say. 'I like girls.'

That was two years ago. Too long ago. Now whisky scorches your mouth. You return to the garage where the air is blue and kind and suddenly it's easy. You're back in there, in the driving seat, going nowhere.

A Fantastic Life
Jon Ronson

It is a Friday in December. I have now been dressed as
Santa for five hours. The heating in our house is on
full blast. The costume was itchy when I put it on all
those hours ago. Now I feel as if I am covered in ants.

'I need to take the beard off,' I say.

'No!' yells Joel, my four-year-old son.

'I'm getting a rash,' I say.

'Please stay with me, Santa,' says Joel.

The phone rings.

'Don't get it, Santa,' says Joel.

I hear the answer-phone click on.

The original plan – which I had devised during a
lull at breakfast when the conversation momentarily
dried – had been to creep up behind Joel dressed as
Santa. I'd say, 'Ho! Ho! Ho!' We would have a laugh
about it. Then I'd take off the costume and we'd go
back to normal. But it didn't work out that way.
Although Joel knew it was me, he was so thrilled to

have his own Santa that he didn't want it to end. Three hours ago, he whispered, 'Will you stay with me for ever, Santa?'

I replied, 'Yes, I will. For ever and ever and ever.'

'I think I may be allergic to whatever fabric they make the beard out of,' I say now.

'Don't go, Santa,' says Joel. 'Don't leave me.'

I give my wife, Elaine, an imploring look. She shrugs and goes downstairs to the kitchen. She thinks I have nobody to blame for this but myself.

'I think I'm getting hives,' I say. 'I'm feeling very, very claustrophobic.'

'No, Santa, no!' says Joel.

'I need air,' I gasp. 'I need air.'

I am having a panic attack dressed as Santa.

'Prepare yourself because I am going to take the beard off . . . now!' I say. I do. Joel runs from the room in tears. I go upstairs to my office for a cigarette.

In my office I log on to Friends Reunited. I've been doing that a lot lately. A few weeks ago I decided to track down the boys who threw me into Roath Park Lake in Cardiff in the winter of 1983, when I was sixteen. In the middle of the night a couple of Sundays ago, I realized I was still angry about what they did. I found one of the culprits, and emailed to inform him that I am now a successful bestselling author.

He emailed me back within a few hours. He told me that the reason why they threw me in the lake back then was because I was a pain in the arse. He added that the tenor of my email has led him to believe that I haven't changed, and that throwing me in the lake again today would be an appropriate response.

I emailed him back to say I notice from his member notes that he now works in the IT department of some insurance company and that I earn more money than he does.

He has not yet emailed me back.

Touché!

'Santa!' yells Joel from downstairs.

'Coming!' I shout.

The message on the answer-phone is from my mother. She runs a hotel with my father and my brother and his wife – the Nant Ddu Lodge Hotel – in the Brecon Beacons mountain range of mid-Wales. I go home to the hotel every Christmas, and at some point I always manage to say, 'I treat this place just like a hotel,' and it always gets a laugh.

Sometimes, famous people stay at the hotel. My mother always phones to tell me when it happens. When John Cole, the BBC journalist, stayed there, my mother phoned me up and said, 'Guess what? John Cole is staying here. Oh, and he hasn't heard of you.'

A few years ago, when John Birt was the Director General of the BBC, he came in for lunch. My father approached his table.

'Are you John Birt?' he asked.

'Yes,' said John Birt.

'I wonder if you can help,' said my father. 'The TV reception in this area can be all crackly and fuzzy. Can you do anything about this?'

I think my father wanted John Birt to get on to the roof and fix the aerial.

'We spoke about all sorts,' my father told me on the phone afterwards. 'The problems I'm having with my car – he couldn't believe that it's been in the garage six times.'

'Oh, and he hasn't heard of you,' added my mother, on the extension line.

Recently, my family won the coveted AA Welsh Hotel of the Year competition. It was a big honour, and they've wanted to do something to commemorate the success. So they've decided to commission a portrait painter to immortalize the Ronsons.

'We've decided to have a group family portrait commissioned,' said my mother on the phone. 'A Ronson family portrait to be hung in the bar. Will you be available for a sitting?'

'Certainly,' I said. 'Who's doing it?'

'He's a brilliant but troubled local artist,' she said. 'He did the mural for the new Cardiff multiplex in the Bay. You must have heard of it.'

'No,' I said.

'Oh, come on,' she said. 'It's been in all the papers.'

It turns out that the artist's particular sub-speciality is painting celebrities in classical Renaissance settings – such as Clint Eastwood ascending to heaven surrounded by angels. His loving recreations of celebrities set my parents thinking. So many famous people stay at their hotel. What if the Ronson family portrait was extended to include celebrities?

'Listen to this!' said my mother on the phone the next day. 'We, the family, will be standing in the grounds of the hotel, surrounded by famous people.'

'Which famous people?' I asked. 'You mean, the famous people who've stayed in the hotel?'

'Oh no,' said my mother. 'Any famous people. You have to choose your three famous people by Friday.

We're working on a tight deadline. Send a Polaroid of yourself to the artist, and come up with three famous people, living or dead. Comedians, statesmen, actors, anything.'

'Let me clarify this,' I said.

'There's nothing to clarify,' said my mother.

'Don't you think it may come across as a little self-aggrandizing?' I asked.

'I'm choosing President Kennedy, Gandhi and Churchill,' said my mother. 'Who are you going to choose?'

This is the message now on my answer-phone. Have I come up with my list of three celebrities yet?

I haven't time for this. I am giving Joel the most perfect Christmas imaginable. This is part of my overall strategy to provide him with a constantly enchanting childhood. I don't want to blow my own trumpet, but I think I provide magical moments for Joel in a far more concentrated and unremitting way than my forefathers ever did. I rarely stop, only to go upstairs for cigarettes. This Christmas will be the summit of what is, in fact, a perpetual endeavour.

Outside the school gates, throughout this month, many of the parents have spoken to me of their plans to give their children the most perfect Christmas imaginable. I wonder if I'll bump into any of them in Lapland. Today, one mother looked tense. She told me that her four-year-old son asked her last night if he's going to die.

'What did you say?' I asked her.

'I, uh, said, "You won't ever die,"' she said. 'And then he said, "What about you and Daddy? Will either of you ever die?" And I said, "No. We will never die, either. None of us will ever die."'

She looked at me anxiously.

'You did the right thing,' I told her.

Sometimes I think we are like an amateur bomb-disposal team, forever cutting the wrong wires.

The Lapland brochure says that Joel will take a husky ride, a reindeer ride, a snowmobile ride, a toboggan ride and, finally, meet Santa himself in a snowy cabin in the middle of a pine forest. I am not paying for the trip. I am writing it up as a travel article for the *Guardian*. This means I'll be able to provide Joel with a magical and unforgettable Christmas, do it all for free, and give my son a unique gift too – the gift of fame. The *Guardian* is sending a photographer called Barry Lewis to Lapland to take pictures of Joel with

Santa, et cetera, and he'll be the cover star of the paper's *Weekend* magazine's Christmas edition. We'll keep it and, in years to come, he'll be able to look at it and be impressed that his father was in a position to get him on the front cover of a magazine.

The trip is two days away. As a precursor, I think about taking Joel to Santa's Kingdom at Wembley. The advert makes it look wonderful – a drawing of a shimmering, snowy, chocolate-box village somehow recreated inside Wembley exhibition halls 1 and 2. The official website includes a visitor's diary written by a seven-year-old called Mary T. Moore. She writes: 'December 12, 2002. We all checked in and were given our wristbands, which were bright blue in colour! Elf street was kool. Santa was exactly like he is in all the photos and he does eat too much chocolate. We played in the snowball alley and Mum went shopping.'

Although her diary was written about her 12 December visit, it was posted on santaskingdom.co.uk on 29 November. This is unnerving. Could Mary T. Moore not exist? Such marketing deceits are acceptable in the realms of everyday adult pursuits, but I am trying to construct a perfect Christmas for my four-year-old and I am in no mood to be fucked with. In the absence of an actual foe to protect my son against, I am forever attuned to the possibility of outsiders carelessly puncturing the ambience of constant enchantment that I have created around him. I decide against taking Joel to Santa's Kingdom.

My father phones me.

'Which celebrities are you choosing for the painting?' I ask him.

'Gary Player, Arnold Palmer and Jack Nicklaus,' he says.

'All golfers?' I ask.

'Who are you choosing?' asks my mother on the extension line.

My mind draws a blank. In fact, I begin to panic. I imagine, in hundreds of years' time, notable art historians gathering around the painting making sarcastic comments. I am feeling hostile to the whole idea, a hostility that manifests itself in a lazy choice of celebrities.

'I've decided to go for the Beverley Sisters,' I tell her.

Actually, I have no interest in girl groups of the 1950s, but I do know that the Beverley Sisters all look exactly alike, and my choice is designed to be viewed, by art historians of the future, as an ironic silent protest.

'You can't have the Beverley Sisters,' says my

mother, knowing me well enough to understand all this in an instant.

'How about Sister Sledge?' I ask.

'Are you trying to ruin this?' says my mother.

I relent and opt for my real all-time celebrity hero. 'Randy Newman,' I say.

'Nobody knows what Randy Newman looks like,' she snaps.

In the end we compromise. For eternity, it will be Jon Ronson, Ike and Tina Turner, and Boris Yeltsin.

I decide not to tell Joel that we're going to Lapland. I opt to make it a magical mystery tour instead. In the taxi to the airport, Joel excitedly cross-questions me for clues as to our destination.

'It *is* Body Worlds, isn't it?' he says. 'Hooray! We're finally going to Body Worlds!'

Body Worlds is a museum exhibition of preserved human remains. 'It isn't Body Worlds,' I say.

Joel's face crumbles.

'I want to go to Body Worlds,' he says.

'Listen,' I say, crossly, 'if you're naughty we're going straight into town to see *Stomp* again.'

'No!' yells Joel, genuinely alarmed. 'Not *Stomp* again. Please, not *Stomp* again.'

This threat works for a few minutes. Then he starts again.

'If we don't go to Body Worlds,' he explains, 'I'm going to keep saying "shit".'

'Joel,' I warn, 'we are not going to Body Worlds.'

'You're worse than Jonathan King,' he yells.

The taxi driver peers suspiciously at us in his rear-view mirror. I wish I'd never told Joel that Jonathan King – whose music he admires – is in prison for being naughty to boys.

'Shit!' says Joel.

I resort to the ace in my pack, the one thing that invariably makes Joel behave well.

'*Jesus* wouldn't have said shit,' I say, 'and *Jesus* wouldn't have wanted to go to Body Worlds.'

Joel loves Jesus. I don't know where this came from, but I suspect it might be from a trailer for a cartoon called *The Lamb of God* on the video of *Scooby Doo and the Witch's Ghost*. We are not a religious family. Like many people, I've relinquished pretty much every aspect of Western living that could be described as 'being part of something bigger than myself'. I am not a member of a union. I don't go to synagogue. The only clubs I'm a member of are the gym, where I don't talk to anyone, and the Randy Newman online fan club, which I rarely log on to. When I was a child, my father, like most people of his generation, spread his well of enchantment around the various clubs to which he belonged. He was a little enchanting at the golf club, a little enchanting at the bridge club and a little enchanting at home. But I concentrate the entirety of my enchantment on Joel.

Northern Finnish Lapland, Sunday night. There are five of us. This is a mini-Arctic expedition. There is Sammy, our local guide and driver. There's Barry Lewis, the *Guardian*'s photographer, whose job it is to take a perfect photograph of Joel with Santa for the magazine's front cover. There's Elaine, my wife. There's Joel. And there's me. It is 7.30 p.m. Sammy has just picked us up from Kuusamo airport. We have not yet reached our log cabin in nearby Ruka – our home for the next three nights. Instead, Sammy has driven us to an equipment-hire shop, a hut in a forest, where we are fitted with snowsuits. We run around outside for a few minutes, throwing snow at each other. Joel has never touched real snow before. He is amazed. But the seven-hour journey (two planes and a two-hour connection at Helsinki airport) has tired him out.

'Can I go to bed now?' he asks the assembled adults.

Sammy smiles enigmatically.

'Maybe,' he says, 'there is something more exciting than sleep tonight. Maybe there will be an amazing Christmas adventure.'

'First I'm going to have an amazing sleeping adventure,' says Joel, cheerfully. 'Then I'll have an amazing Christmas adventure tomorrow.'

'Maybe not,' laughs Sammy, 'maybe the adventure will begin tonight.'

I take Sammy to one side. 'What's going on?' I ask.

'Joel must meet Santa tonight!' he whispers, urgently. 'There's a horse-drawn sleigh parked outside your cabin right now, and it's going to take you through the forest to another cabin, and Santa is already there, hidden, waiting for Joel.'

'Bloody hell,' I say.

Joel yawns, happily unaware of the unfolding crisis. Elaine has overheard some of this conversation, and she gives me a panicked stare that says, 'For Christ's sake, get them to postpone Santa.'

'Joel's very tired,' I say. 'Can we not meet Santa in the morning? We're jet-lagged and we need to unpack and acclimatize ourselves.'

'That is impossible,' says Sammy, with startling finality.

There is a silence.

'Perhaps the sight of the horse-drawn sleigh will perk Joel up,' I say.

The five of us climb into the minibus and we drive through the snowy forest. We turn a corner, and all at once we gasp. Our cabin is covered in a blanket of thick snow. The surrounding pine trees glisten with snow, too, and a path of glowing candles lights up the driveway. A horse-drawn sleigh, complete with jingle bells and reindeer pelts, waits for us at the front door, as does the sleigh's driver. It is just about the loveliest thing I have ever seen.

'Bedtime!' yells Joel.

He jumps out of the van, ignoring the one-horse open sleigh, and rushes, focused, into the warm cabin. I follow him inside. He has already found a double bed and has jumped into it, pulling the duvet up to his chin.

'This is a perfect bed,' he says. 'Good night.'

'I think,' I say, 'that somebody very special wants to meet you before you go to sleep.'

Joel thinks about this for a moment.

'No,' he says.

I hurry outside.

'Sammy,' I say, 'we have a serious problem. Joel is already almost asleep. He's only four.'

'We do have a serious problem,' says Sammy, 'because Santa is only available immediately.'

Barry the photographer intercedes.

'Do you really want a picture of a scared, tired and crying child meeting Santa?' he asks.

'No,' says Sammy, 'but the schedule is inflexible.'

I notice, in the darkness behind the cabin, figures moving around. I don't know who they are. I assume they are shadowy cogs in this apparently complicated operation.

I rush over to Elaine. 'They're not backing down!' I hiss.

'Oh God,' says Elaine.

'I'm not coming out,' yells Joel from the window.

I rush back inside.

'The horse is crying,' I tell Joel, 'because he's dying to meet you. He's crying now!'

There is a silence.

'OK,' he says, 'I'll meet the horse. But that's it. Then I'm going straight back to bed.'

Together, Joel and I walk out into the snow.

'Hello,' says Joel magnanimously to the horse.

'Joel,' says Sammy, 'would you like to sit in the sleigh for a moment while you talk to the horse?'

Joel shoots Sammy a suspicious glance. Nonetheless, he climbs into the sleigh. I quickly jump in and throw a reindeer pelt over the two of us. Elaine and Barry pile hurriedly in behind us.

'Go!' I hiss. 'Go!'

The driver cracks the whip, and the horse trots lazily off down the snowy lane towards Santa. We fall into a wonderful silence. The jingle bells ring out magically with every step the horse takes. A stirring of northern lights pulsates above us as we ride through the shimmering pine trees. Joel's mood is lifted. He begins to sing 'Jingle Bells' to himself.

'It's just so beautiful,' I sigh. 'Isn't it, Joel? Isn't it perfect?'

Joel doesn't answer.

Behind me, Elaine and Barry begin to bitch incessantly.

'Would it have been too much to have asked for a negotiable timetable?' mutters Barry.

'It's just a nightmare,' agrees Elaine.

Barry and Elaine are working themselves up into something of a frenzy, out here in the shimmering pine forest.

'People bring terminally ill children here,' says Elaine. 'You don't force a terminally ill child to meet Santa.'

'That's completely right,' says Barry.

We park up outside a log cabin and walk inside to discover that a vast banquet has been laid on for us. Joel takes one look at the meats and cookies and juice and salmon platter and he bursts into tears. 'You tricked me,' he wails, throwing himself underneath a pine bench and adopting a foetal position.

During crisis situations such as this, I usually attempt to alter Joel's mood by transforming myself into some kind of physical comedian, pulling out all the stops to provide instant enchantment. I use any prop to hand, interspersing my slapstick buffoonery by yelling out positive statements such as, 'You're extremely talented, Joel! You're going to be a great success in later life!'

Instead, I whisper to Sammy, 'If Santa comes right now we may be OK.'

Sammy and I hurry outside to find a lovely old Santa, his eyes twinkling, rubbing his hands to keep warm inside a four-wheel drive parked behind a tree.

'Hello!' he hollers.

'Let's do it now, Santa,' I say.

'OK!' says Santa.

I rush back to the cabin and dramatically fling open the door. Joel, noticing an escape opportunity, squeezes out from underneath the bench and makes a run for it, just as Santa appears from the darkness. Joel skids to a startled halt.

'Ho! Ho! Ho!' says Santa.

'Get them to stand next to each other,' urges Barry the photographer. 'I can't get them in the same frame.'

Santa takes a step towards Joel. Joel takes an anxious step backwards.

'He's demented with exhaustion,' whispers Elaine through gritted teeth.

'You're the best, Santa!' I holler as loudly as I can, trying to drown out all the negativity.

'They look like they're in different rooms,' mutters Barry, panicked. 'Joel! Do you think there's a mouse living in Santa's beard? Would you like to go and look?'

'This is making me very sad,' says Elaine.

'Oh, Santa, I'm so tired,' says Joel, giving him an imploring look, as if to say, 'If anyone can stop this madness, surely you can.'

'We all love you, Santa,' I screech.

Randy Newman was once asked about a song of his, 'I Love to See You Smile', the title theme to the movie *Parenthood*.

'It's the most lucrative song I ever wrote,' he said. 'I was able to hire a nanny to play with my children for me. So a movie about being a good parent allowed me to put even more distance between my children and myself.'

I think about this as I attempt to coerce the exhausted and hugely reluctant Joel towards Santa so Barry can get a decent photograph to accompany my travel article, which will earn me enough money to pay for Joel's nanny for another eight weeks. Then I shrug and think, 'Things have gone too far to stop now,' and I ask Joel if he can spot the mouse in Santa's beard.

'Peace and quiet at last,' says Joel, back in his bed in the log cabin.

'Wasn't Santa lovely?' I say, trying to gauge the level of emotional scarring Joel has suffered in the past hour. Actually, he was a great Santa, a perfect Santa, unfazed by the chaos. Things did settle down after a while, with Joel telling Santa that his bedroom is the one with the two *Harry Potter* posters so he'll know where to leave the presents. But now, in bed, Joel's mind is on other things. He's thinking about a boy who is apparently something of a class bully. Two days before we set off for Lapland, by Joel's account, this boy shouted at him. In bed, Joel suddenly sits up and says, 'I'm going to have a horrible life.'

I gasp. 'No you're not,' I say. 'You're going to have a fantastic life. Do you know why?'

'Why?' Joel asks.

'Because you're clever and funny,' I say. 'Clever, funny people have fantastic lives.'

Joel allows himself a small, optimistic smile. Elaine listens, unnoticed by me, from the doorway.

'In fact,' I add, pleased that I'm doing so well, 'do you know which people have horrible lives after leaving school? Bullies! Bullies leave school and have horrible lives, while special people like you have blessed, magical lives, where nothing bad happens at all.'

'Really?' asks Joel.

'Yes,' I say. 'Only bad things happen to bullies, and only good things happen to people like you.'

'Those were the worst bloody words of wisdom I've heard in my life,' shouts Elaine, furiously, later.

'What?' I say.

'First,' says Elaine, 'Joel won't automatically have a fantastic life. In fact, he'll probably have a worse life now because of the unrealistic expectations you've just instilled in him.'

'Oh, God,' I say, horrified. 'He'll forget I said it, won't he?'

'And bullies don't automatically have terrible lives,'

adds Elaine. 'What you just told Joel was warped and disturbing. You're teaching the boy *schadenfreude*!'

Before Joel was born, I had a mental picture of what fatherhood might be like: my son and I were in a car together, driving down a motorway. We turned to each other and smiled. That was it. I notice now that this mental picture lacked dialogue. I had no idea what we might actually say to each other. In this mental picture, neither one of us said or did anything that might screw the other one up.

Joel is too excited to sleep. Elaine, Barry and I drink cognac in front of the fire while Joel bounces around in front of us.

'Shit!' he sings, screeching across the room. 'Shit! Shit! Shit!'

'Peter, Susan, Edmund and Lucy didn't say shit in Narnia,' I say.

'You're good at the humour,' says Barry, who has raised four children, 'but a weakness in your parenting is control. Control is the weak spot.'

'Do you really think I'm good at the humour?' I ask, flattered.

'Yes,' says Barry.

'You said that in such a way as to imply that being good at the humour isn't enough,' I say.

Barry looks at me to see if I'm joking. When he realizes I'm not, he gives me a brief, pitying stare, and says nothing about my parenting skills again.

The next day my mother calls me on my mobile phone to ask if we're having a nice time in Lapland. She also wants me to know that she's spoken with the artist to tell him that the concept for the family portrait has changed again. Each Ronson is no longer to be standing and chatting to the celebrities. We're going to be serving them drinks. This is, after all, a hotel.

'So now I'm to be frozen in time in an act of subservience,' I say, 'to Boris Yeltsin?'

'It's just a bloody painting,' says my mother.

Is there really such a thing as 'just a painting'? Paintings are permanent, powerful things. So are photographs. The people portrayed within them are no longer in control. They become something else, whatever the photographer, or the artist, or the viewer, wants them to be. I tell my mother that I'll speak to her when we get home, and I hang up. I look over at Barry, who is making coffee. He seems worried. He says he never got a perfect shot of Joel and Santa together. When Sammy arrives to pick us up, Barry asks him if the organization can broker another meeting between them, this time with more advance warning.

Sammy is concerned.

'But any Santa we manage to get now won't be the real Santa,' he says.

'Uh . . .' I say.

'Yes, yes,' says Sammy, cutting my obvious next question short. He reluctantly agrees to find a Santa to meet us at the reindeer farm tomorrow.

The next twenty-four hours are blissful. Sammy takes us husky sleighing. We drink reindeer soup in a tepee in a frozen forest. We end the day with a snowmobile expedition across a frozen lake. Joel sits on Sammy's bike, curled up between his legs. Joel has become besotted with Sammy. The next morning, Sammy drives us to a reindeer farm. The reindeer takes Joel and me on a hair-raising sleigh ride across a field, kicking snow in Joel's face.

'That's IT!' yells Joel, giving the reindeer and me a ferocious stare as if to say, 'I know the two of you plotted this together.'

I wipe the snow from Joel's face.

'I'm going to have a horrible life,' says Joel.

The reindeer farmer's son, who can speak little English, disappears at lunchtime. He reappears a few moments later dressed as Santa – a tall, skinny, surly Santa.

'Look, Joel!' says Barry, raising his camera. 'Wow! How about that?'

'Hello again, Santa.' Joel laughs excitedly. 'I didn't know you were coming to see me again.'

Santa nods, grumpily.

'I wonder if Santa has got a mouse living in his beard?' says Barry.

'It's lovely to see you,' says Joel.

Santa silently folds his arms, diffidently tapping his fingers against his coat.

'Santa?' says Joel, concerned. 'Are you OK?'

'Santa has reindeer problems,' I say. 'Isn't that true, Santa? You've come to check on your reindeers because they're sick, that's why you're preoccupied.'

Santa grunts. Barry gets a lovely photograph of Joel posing with Santa.

Twenty-four hours later, and we're back in London. Joel's nanny, Francielly, is feeding the cat. She's there when we arrive home. Joel runs through the front door.

'Our log cabin,' he shrieks, 'had two toilets.'

'Really?' says Francielly.

'Two toilets!' sighs Joel, contentedly.

Months pass. My father telephones the artist from time to time to find out how things are going with the family portrait and when is he likely to be finished? Most often, the artist doesn't even pick up, and when he does he's a man of few words, which are spoken gruffly.

'Nearly there,' he says.

'Are you pleased with it so far?' asks my father.

'Don't worry,' says the artist.

My father begins to worry.

The concept has changed yet again. My mother has decided – and has informed the artist – that we won't be serving drinks to the celebrities after all. Instead, we'll be talking and the celebrities will be listening. We are, after all, the hotel's hosts.

'So you'll be talking,' I clarify, 'and Kennedy, Gandhi and Churchill will be listening?'

'What's the problem?' says my mother.

'Nothing,' I say. 'I'm just worried that people may get the wrong idea. You know, that we consider our-selves as good as Kennedy and—'

'What are you saying?' says my mother.

'Nothing,' I say. 'What will you be talking about to Kennedy, Gandhi and Churchill?'

'What do you mean, what will I be talking to them about?' says my mother. 'Nothing. I'm talking to them about nothing. It's a painting.'

'Maybe Dad will be talking to the golfers about the amount of times his car has been in the garage,' I suggest.

The day of the grand unveiling comes without warning. The artist just turns up one morning carrying a large canvas covered in a white sheet. He props it up against the bar. The family gather around it with a sense of great expectation. Everyone looks at the covered painting and at the artist, trying to scrutinize his facial expression. It is, well, troubled.

The artist says, 'I think you ought to know that I'm going through a creative stage that some people find difficult to connect to.'

There is a nervous silence.

'What I'm saying,' he continues, 'is there's a possibility you may not like it.'

The Ronsons look anxiously at one another. Then, with a flourish, the artist whips off the sheet.

'There you go,' he says.

For a moment, the Ronsons just stare. My mother whispers, 'Oh my God.' She yelps quietly, and storms out of the room. My brother and his wife follow, as a show of unity, slamming the door behind them.

The artist is left alone with my father. They don't make eye contact. They just stare at the painting.

The famous people have all been painted with tender accuracy. There are a few celebrities – Clint Eastwood, Rowan Atkinson and Jennifer Saunders – whom none of the Ronsons have actually asked for, and many of the celebrities the Ronsons had requested are missing.

But that isn't the problem. The problem is that although the celebrities are lovingly depicted, the Ronsons stand among them as human grotesqueries, repulsive caricatures of monsters. My brother looks like Frankenstein. He has a bolt through his neck. It is disturbing and humiliating. My parents look like hastily sketched recovering drug addicts. I look like a gawky, spotty adolescent, frozen in a gormless pose. But, unlike the other Ronsons, at least it does look a bit like me.

The painter has spent all those months making the celebrities look beatific, and he's just whipped off the Ronsons really fast, as though he's done us the night before as a hostile afterthought. Plus, the Ronsons are utterly dwarfed by the celebrities – my brother is a small Frankenstein, peeking out behind Clint Eastwood's shoulder.

'Sorry,' says the painter, looking at the floor.

'We're not paying for it,' says my father.

There is a long silence.

'It's just not, um, realistic enough,' says my father, attempting something conciliatory, as if the original idea of serving mint juleps to John F. Kennedy and Robert Mitchum was more realistic.

My father orders the artist to paint the Ronsons out and, after much negotiation, he agrees. He turns my mother into Woody Allen. That's kind of humiliating in itself – that the easiest brush-over will render her as Woody Allen. My father is now Jimmy Carter. I like to think the artist chose Jimmy Carter, the famed peacemaker, to replace my dad as a homage to my father's diplomacy – because he was the only Ronson who didn't storm out. My brother is turned into David Rockefeller and his wife is turned into Henry Kissinger, which I interpret as an act of hostility. The only Ronson left in the portrait is, oddly, me.

The painting now hangs in the smoking lounge next to the bistro in my family's hotel, and it is the cause of much interest among the customers. They crowd around it, trying to guess who everyone is.

'That's Kennedy!' they say. 'Look, Jennifer Saunders.'

Nobody gets David Rockefeller. I have to say, 'It's David Rockefeller.'

'Ah,' they reply, 'David Rockefeller.'

They stare blankly at the likeness of me, too, for whole minutes at a time, trying to figure out who exactly I am.

'I'm an author,' I say.

But they all just squint and shrug.

The laws of physics tell us that one needs to be very careful approaching a star. If your trajectory and speed are just right, you'll go into orbit, safe and sound, glowing in the warm, beautiful starlight. If you mess up in any way – the wrong direction, the wrong speed – you'll hurtle into the face of the star and be vaporized; only the star will remain.

I've kept the magazine with the cover photograph of Joel in Lapland, just in case he may want to see it one day in the future. When I look closely at it I can see that Joel – although smiling – has something of a thousand-yard stare about him. When I look at the painting in my family's hotel, and at the snowy Lapland photograph, I realize that I can never write about Joel again.

Rape Semantics
Alice Sebold

My rapist's parole hearing was held the day before I returned to the city of Syracuse. Fifteen years earlier I had been raped in Thorden Park, near the Syracuse University campus. The rapist, a man I'll call Gregory Madison, was convicted on six of seven counts with which he was indicted by a grand jury, but the fact that he was still in jail amazed everyone I knew. I was eighteen and a virgin at the time of the attack. He was twenty-two and well known to the police. Now I was thirty-three and he was thirty-seven. I was returning to Syracuse to meet up with the assistant district attorney on the case. She had offered to drive up from Utica, where she now worked, to meet me for breakfast, and then shepherd me through the evidence box that, with a few phone calls to her old cronies, she had been able to locate and have held until I could make arrangements to fly out from California.

As my partner and I drove the rent-a-car to the

Rape Semantics

Holiday Inn near the campus where, fifteen years earlier, my mother had been staying overnight when she
got the call that I had been raped and beaten, the low
sky of Syracuse began to turn from its usual grey to a
more ominous blue-grey. It was mid-August and the
humidity had been building up to this point all day.
We drove off the highway overpass and into the city
streets just as a drizzle started falling. We parked in
the overhead parking structure and registered in the
hotel lobby. By the time we reached our room on the
15th floor, hammerhead clouds were massing in the
sky. A few minutes later, the build-up reached breaking point and what had seemed benign showers burst
into the kind of late-summer thunder and lightning
storm that I'd left fifteen years earlier. We opened the
blinds to watch it. We could see the whole city – or the
part of it that had been my city – from Thorden Park
through the campus and all the way to the grittier side
of the overpass where the Public Safety Building and
the Onondaga Courtroom Building lay. I explained to
Glen, a California native, that yes, it was always like
this – a grey dome covered the city both rain and
shine. My head was throbbing. I had kept at bay the
idea that Gregory Madison could be on the streets the
same day I came back. I went into the bathroom and

when I came out, Glen was on the phone. 'Yes, I'll tell her,' he said. 'Yes, thank you.'

I looked at him. Gregory Madison had been denied parole. My former assistant district attorney knew how important it would be for me to hear it. We celebrated with horrible hotel wine and sat in darkness, watching the rain.

I have thought of Gregory Madison, ever since we met in a park at night, as my husband. What I mean by this is that at an age when I was nursing innocent crushes for boys my age, a stranger I didn't know violently possessed me. He and it – the experience of rape – were the most vivid experience I'd ever had and one I knew immediately I owed a debt to. What I owed, was trying to articulate what rape was, and how it felt and, by pointing at myself, to try and demystify it for my peers and elders. To make it what I pretended it was for years – a big deal that was no big deal.

I blurted the facts of it, drunkenly, to fellow students and very, very soberly in a variety of courtroom appearances. I wrote horrible poems about it in creative writing classes and I 'fictionalized' it in a musical comedy review called *Rape!*. Every boy, then man, I dated had to pass the test of whether they could handle it, and every book I picked up had to deal with it in a way I thought of as the right way. I would not burn a book, but I boiled *The Book of Laughter and Forgetting* on my stove top during my senior year in college, I threw the 'Raj Quartet' out the window of the M101 bus in New York, and I was stunned at the portrayal of the rape in *The World According to Garp*. I was stunned because it had been written by a man.

I liked this last fact, and I clung to it. Anything that didn't fit the stereotype was what I wanted. Rape victims got fat. I would not get fat. Rape victims were celibate. I would not be celibate. Rape victims hated men. I would cherish them. Rape victims were full of fear. I was numb to it. And I stayed on this course for years, defining myself as much in reaction to the stereotypes as any woman (or man) defines themselves by them.

Perhaps the rule of being raped that I broke the most was being quiet about it. I told everyone, given the chance, because I thought people needed to know what I called 'the score'. I look back now and I think the way I told some poor souls is akin to the way my father tried to discipline a dog we once had. He would take this animal and rub his nose in his own mistake until the thing couldn't breathe. What good it did was none, but my father remained convinced that this was a procedure that would exact results. It did. The dog hated him.

People thought I was lying. They thought I was pitiful. They thought I was cool. They thought I was tough or weird, or crazy. On occasion a woman would say, 'You mean you're a rape survivor', stressing this last word as if enamelling over some unpleasant patch. When this happened, my narrative ceased and I would stare.

'I'm a rape victim.'

'The term is rape survivor,' many well-intentioned people would correct.

The morning after Glen and I sat and watched the rain, Gail, my old assistant district attorney who now works for a judge, met us for breakfast in the Holiday Inn dining room. All I wanted was coffee. I had the shakes as I had last time I'd seen her – the day of my testimony. She was already there when we arrived, as tall as I remembered but with long wavy hair now instead of the short and functional style she'd worn then. She was smiling ear to ear and though I was thirty-three she still called me 'Kiddo' when she hugged me.

'I brought something,' she said. 'Do you remember this?'

Out of her large patent-leather purse she drew a

dog-eared yellow cow that my mother and I had gone shopping for in 1981. Gail was pregnant during my trial and hadn't been able to try my case because the defence had thought her pregnancy would prove prejudicial. She sat behind the prosecutors' table as the district attorney questioned me.

She sent me a birth announcement, one of the few bright spots in a large blue folder that first had a label that said 'Rape 1981–82' and then was changed after my best friend was raped in an apartment we shared. I crossed out the years.

I had coffee and Gail and Glen made conversation. 'I have no idea what's in this evidence box. Are you up for it, Glen?'

Glen was. I had asked him to come. At some point on that trip of under twenty-four hours, we drove through the campus where I'd been a student and into the park where I'd been raped. I asked him to stay in the car and I walked over a slight hill to stare down at the tunnel where it had begun. Without telling me, he took two pictures through the window. I am glad to have them now and keep them with the 8 x 10 copies of the evidence photos from my trial.

The three of us made our way to the building that housed the district attorney's office, Gail keeping up cheery banter all the way; something I now remembered she'd done throughout the pre-trial hearings, the grand jury, the line-up, the night before the trial itself. It had an odd effect on me. It made me keep on walking. I had to use part of my energy to try and focus on the somewhat immaterial talk and by doing this I was unable to be overwhelmed by where I was and what I was doing. It had worked then and it worked now. What did she say? I can't remember. But we were inside, in an elevator, and then on the floor where the assistant district attorneys bustled around and phones rang shrilly over partitions that were far from ergonomic in the current style.

It was old home week for Gail. People she hadn't seen for years – all men, it seemed – asked her what she was doing back in her 'old stomping grounds', 'this neck of the woods', and accused her good-naturedly of 'slumming'. Though she addressed everyone, she also led us with little dally time to the office of her friend, the attorney who had stored the evidence box for so many months.

I was wound up and so was Glen. I was being intro-duced to people as the victim in the rape case of New York vs. Madison from 1981. The men had to take in that I was a victim then – not now – adjust themselves accordingly, hark back fifteen years to remember the case – a rare success and so not impossible – all the while trying to enjoy a light-hearted moment with an old colleague in the midst of a day that included many cases that would be far less successful than mine.

I was also proud to shake their hands. I was that rape victim and as odd as it may sound, I was proud to be recognized as such. My success on the stand had been the major achievement of my life up to the point I turned nineteen, yet I'd never been able to share this fact with a group who knew what it meant, and who didn't need to make sure I was okay or have 'what is rape' explained.

Just as the three of us entered her friend's office and he was standing up from his desk to greet us, we heard a female voice.

'My best friend was the victim in the Madison case!'

I turned around and so did Gail and Glen, to see a heavy-set woman with glasses and ringlets enter the room. The only way I can describe how she looked is to say that she had arrived in that room to claim a prize.

I stared at her; Gail and Glen kind of stepped to the side. All I could think was what Glen later confided was going through his head too: Madison raped someone else that same year?

'Alice Sebold is my best friend,' this woman said

and then she must have realized. Or was it that Gail, choosing wisely, addressed me by my first name?

The moment was awkward now. Gail's old cronies stood behind the woman. Gail's friend was still waiting to be introduced. I froze. I was there to look at an evidence box.

Then the woman caught herself in the only way she could. She rushed forward and embraced me. 'Oh Alice, it's so good to see you,' she said. 'How are you?' She shoved her card in my hand and implored me to call her, then went away. She was an assistant district attorney.

A few minutes later, as we sat alone in the room and prepared to open the box, Gail said, 'You have no idea who she was, have you?'

I stared at the card. 'No,' I said.

In the box was much of what I'd come for. Gail went through it first and made legal decisions – what I could and could not see. I had already ordered a copy of the trial via mail and so I knew that it had been my own testimony, physical evidence and Madison's own testimony that had sealed my rapist's fate. But to see his handwritten appeals from prison, to see some of the things he claimed of me, to see the lists of crimes for which he had been a suspect – most notably the killing of an elderly black woman choked to death on her parakeet. Madison had been convicted as a juvenile of robbing this same woman and he and his accomplice were suspected of finally losing control.

My mind reeled. Gail kept going. 'This isn't germane. Do you want a copy of this? Get a load of this jerk, he claimed you stated you wanted sex! Oh, this is priceless, he had gout and that's how he got out of the service. Let's get a copy of this affidavit. Do you have this?'

Glen held the documents I wanted copies of. Gail sat in the middle, weeding, plucking, deciding. 'Nope, not this,' she said, and I watched papers I would have loved to get a look at be placed upside down in her lap.

And then she stopped. She was holding onto a manila envelope. 'Okay,' she said, 'these are the photos.' She looked at me and then at Glen a second later. 'There will be photos of the scene, photos of you and photos of him in here. Are you ready?'

I said I was. Glen nodded. He had been scribbling notes down the whole time in a notebook – I had asked him to be a second set of eyes. Now he stopped.

The tunnel came first – a tunnel that led to an outdoor amphitheatre which had since then been sealed at one end with iron doors. I passed it to Glen. He sat stunned. Then there were photos of the ground surrounding the tunnel where I had struggled. A photo with my broken glasses and a knife half open beside them. When he had threatened me and gone for the knife, I had kicked him and it never, to my eyes, materialized. Then there was a photo of him – or more precisely of the line-up in which he stood. They lined them up in the hall outside and took this shot. He was wearing the same style of shoes he'd been wearing the night he'd raped me. I didn't really look at this one. I asked my question: 'Can I get copies?' Gail said she would look into it. I knew I'd have to be alone to really stare at the photo the way I needed to, unseen by other eyes.

But what I had not prepared for was seeing the photos of myself.

There are four. A close-up of a bruise on my neck where he attempted to strangle me when I screamed. Two close-ups of my face where he'd punched me and gouged his nails into my nose and cheeks. But it is the last one that I still have trouble looking at. I am standing with my identifying case number written hurriedly across a Public Safety Building envelope. I am wearing clothes my freshman-year girlfriends found and brought to the hospital that same night. My eyes are not closed as they are in the other photos where a policeman had cautioned me to do this in order to avoid the bright flash since he was so close to my face. My eyes are looking downward to no particular point – what soldiers call the thousand-yard stare. The only thing I can say is that mine bore a mantle of incredible shame. It was the violence, yes, the brutality, but it was the sex used as a weapon that brought the shame. I was a rape victim in those photos. Though I have survived, I am a rape victim still, just as friends of mine, now sober, are alcoholics, just like the men who served in Vietnam are still Vets. It is an unchangeable – by semantics or good intention – reality. Words are curtains behind which we cannot hide.

For weeks after that trip I kept saying aloud the name of the woman who had hugged me. I questioned Mary Alice, who was my best friend when this woman claimed to know me, but she had no clue. I described her physically.

We thought it might be a girl who lived on our hall.

But finally I remembered her. She was in a poetry class I took, taught by Hayden Carruth. I'd written a political poem about men raping women in wartime, and Carruth had bawled me out, used the 'write what you know' theorem and condemned the poem. Someone must have told him because, later, he apologized repeatedly. In the class had been this quiet girl who barely spoke but, as I recall it, she loved Emily Dick-inson and wanted to write like her.

On the last night, one of the students brought in home-made wine. I had more than my fair share and threw up in the file drawer of a secretary. I had to be taken home. It was this girl and someone else, a boy, who stood on either side of me and led me back to my dorm. I was in the midst of the trial preparations. I was a mess all the way round.

Outside Bird Library we stopped to rest and then it came – the sound of an ambulance cresting the hill in its descent to Crouse Irving Hospital. I started screaming, and fell to the ground. They tried to hush me but I was lost to them, curling up in a foetal posi-tion on the cold winter pavement of Syracuse and holding my hands to my ears. I don't remember how they managed it, but the next morning I woke up in my dorm room. Safe. There was a note by my bed. 'Hope you are all right. Please call me. Please take care of yourself. Please.' It was written by this woman who claimed me fifteen years later and whom I could-n't, until now, recognize.

About a year before I published my memoir in the States, I had a premonition, but I didn't call the one person who I knew might confirm it. I was busy trying to write about the rape and needed to finish my work before I contacted Gail. When I did, it only took her a day to make the calls and get the answer.

Gregory Madison would be released on parole in six months – at the start of 1999. I used to tell a lot of bad jokes in the years immediately following my rape. It was an effort to both win friends and comfort them. I had a new one then, 'Madison and Sebold both out in 99.' I think it's pretty funny, actually. I know it covers a lot of pain.

I am a rape victim and he is my rapist. No matter how well-intentioned, it would be a lie to call us by any other name.

Acknowledgements

With thanks to Peter Straus, who provided the initial encouragement for this book, and Imogen Taylor and Andrew Kidd, who made it happen. Thanks, too, to Ed Victor, for his patience and advice, and Camilla Elworthy, William Fiennes, Jon Ronson and Nick Hornby, who were all unfailingly generous with their thoughts on memoir in general, and this book in particular.

Part of Nick Hornby's piece was originally broadcast in the US on *This American Life*, 2000.

Author Biographies

ANDREA ASHWORTH is the author of a memoir, *Once In a House On Fire* (Picador), and is currently writing her next book. She lives in California.

RACHEL CUSK has written four novels and a memoir, *A Life's Work: On Becoming a Mother* (Fourth Estate); her most recent novel is *The Lucky Ones* (Fourth Estate/Perennial). She lives in Bristol.

SOPHIE DAHL is a model and is the author of *The Man with the Dancing Eyes* (Bloomsbury). She lives in New York and is currently writing a novel.

SABINE DURRANT is a journalist, and the author of two novels, *Having It and Eating It* and *The Great Indoors*, both published by TimeWarner. She lives in London.

Author Biographies

WILLIAM FIENNES is the author of a travel memoir, *The Snow Geese* (Picador), and is writing his second book. He lives in Oxfordshire.

ESTHER FREUD is the author of five novels, including *Hideous Kinky* and most recently *The Sea House* (Viking Penguin). She lives in London.

ZOE HELLER is a journalist and the author of two novels, *Everything You Know* and, most recently, *Notes on a Scandal* (Viking Penguin). She lives in New York.

NICK HORNBY is the author of *Fever Pitch, High Fidelity, About A Boy* and *How To Be Good* (VikingPenguin), and has recently published a non-fiction book about music, *31 Songs* (Penguin). He lives in London.

JULIE MYERSON is the author of five novels, including *Something Might Happen* (Vintage), and has recently published a non-fiction work, *Home: The Story Of Everyone Who Ever Lived In Our House* (Flamingo). She lives in London.

JON RONSON is a journalist, film maker and author of two non-fiction books, *Them: Adventures with*

Author Biographies

Extremists (Picador) and *The Men who Stare at Goats* (Picador). He lives in London.

ALICE SEBOLD is the author of a memoir, *Lucky* (Picador), and a novel, *The Lovely Bones* (Picador). She lives in California.